Rebels in go

Manchester University Press

Rebels in government

Is Sinn Féin ready for power?

Agnès Maillot

Manchester University Press

Published by Manchester University Press
Oxford Road, Manchester M13 9PL
www.manchesteruniversitypress.co.uk

British Library Cataloguing-in-Publication Data
A catalogue record for this book is available from the British Library

ISBN 978 1 5261 5454 5 hardback
ISBN 978 1 5261 5456 9 paperback

First published 2022

Typeset
by Cheshire Typesetting Ltd, Cuddington, Cheshire
Printed in Great Britain
by TJ Books, Ltd

Contents

Figures and tables

Figure

Tables

Acknowledgements

I would like to thank all those who made the writing of this book possible, including: Siobhan Fenton, Sinn Féin press officer, for her help in procuring most of the interviews contained in this book; all the interviewees for taking the time to talk and to share their experiences and analyses; Bairbre Ní Chiosáin, Mathieu Doogan, Lily Lee and Laurent Marie for their invaluable proofreading and feedback.

And last but not least, Rémi, Samuel and Chloé for their continued support.

Abbreviations

DUP   Democratic Unionist Party
GFA   Good Friday Agreement
IRA   Irish Republican Army
MLA   Member of the Local Assembly
PSNI   Polics Service of Northern Ireland
RIC   Royal Irish Constabulary
SDLP   Social Democratic Labour Party
TD   Teachta Dála (member of Dáil Éireann)
UUP   Ulster Unionist Party

Introduction

After many years of relentless efforts to make a break-through in Irish politics, Sinn Féin's strategy eventually paid off in the February 2020 general election. Winning a high share of the popular vote, which even the campaign strategists had not anticipated, the party showed it had gained the confidence of a sizeable section of the electorate. Sinn Féin's success seemed to take the Irish political scene by surprise. While opinion polls had indeed tracked its progress in the run-up to polling day, the breadth and scope of the support for a party that most in the Dáil still saw as an outlier in the Irish political system were less predictable, particularly in light of the electoral decline that Sinn Féin had experienced the previous year, on both sides of the border, at local and EU elections. However, while its respectability was still questioned in some quarters, Sinn Féin had now secured its place as a potential coalition partner in future governments, a role it has been playing in Northern Ireland since the start of the century. However, the prospect of this all-Ireland, radical left and former Provisional IRA associate being in government raises many questions. To what extent will this impact the prospect of reunification? Have its connections with the IRA been properly severed, and is the party as democratic as it claims to be? What do the radical changes that the party advocates, in areas such as housing, public health and taxation, say about a party whose ideology has meandered so much throughout the twentieth century?

Sinn Féin's breakthrough was neither unpredictable nor an error in history. The party has shown a capacity to make an entrance into Irish politics when the times are ripe. Several factors account for this: its strong and centralised organisation; its capacity to adapt to circumstances, whether adverse or favourable; its commitment to key issues that give continuity to its discourse; its sense of strategy and its grassroots approach; and its vitality and energy, reflected in both the youth of its membership and candidates, and in the age group which it attracts amongst voters.

This does not, however, mean that the route the party embarked upon at the start of the twenty-first century was a smooth one. It was predicated on a number of political gambles, most of which are still unresolved. Is reunification really desirable, and will the party be able to convince public opinion on both sides of the border? Has the party entirely shed its darker and more controversial alter ego, the IRA? Is a radical left-wing approach to social issues, which directly contradicts the very make-up of Irish politics, the best possible approach in the age of globalisation and neoliberalism?

A brief look at the headlines of the international media in the aftermath of the 2020 general election indicates how intriguing Sinn Féin remains to a large section of international opinion, with grandiose and hyperbolic expressions used to describe what the editors seemed at a loss to comprehend. Thus, headlines such as 'Shock result', 'Political earthquake', 'Historic result', 'Tsunami', 'Seismic shock' abounded, with CNN trying to explain 'why that's so controversial'. But those headlines do capture the profound repercussions of the rise of a party that is such an anomaly in the European political context. Of course, the unmistakable left-turn that the electorate was signalling by voting for a party that put forward a programme for radical change in terms of social policy was noteworthy in a country that had until then seemed comfortable with a neoliberal and rather conservative agenda. Similarly, the party's very history and its former ties with the IRA also account for the prediction that this result could potentially have disrupted the political status quo in Ireland, by putting an end to the two-party dominance. Finally, and perhaps most importantly, the prospect that the Sinn Féin vote opened for Irish unity was noted by most publications.

While all these diagnostics raised interesting questions, they mainly rested on the fact that Sinn Féin would indeed access the levers of power and be part of the next government, although anyone with a cursory knowledge of Irish political life could have predicted that this would not happen that easily. Sinn Féin in government is an option that neither Fianna Fáil nor Fine

Gael – the dominant parties in the Irish political land-scape until February 2020 – had ever considered, and they had repeatedly signalled that this would not be a scenario they would entertain. What those results did indicate was a willingness on the part of the electorate not to heed the warnings, repeated over the years, that Sinn Féin was still somehow linked to the IRA and that it could not be trusted on this point, or any other for that matter.

The question of reunification was also raised by some media pundits, with the *Economist* going as far as to venture that 'Irish unification is becoming likelier' (*Economist*, A United Ireland: Could it really happen? 15/02/20). Evidently, this dimension could not be under-estimated when analysing the significance of Sinn Féin's success. Indeed, at the core of the party's identity, ideol-ogy, strategies and *raison d'être* is Irish unity. This is what underlies strategic decisions, campaigns and most policy programmes. It is what links all the different versions of a party that has experienced multiple splits, several changes of direction, even spectacular U-turns in terms of policy orientation. Reunification is what drives its dis-course, but this is also, to a large extent, what makes Sinn Féin a unique party within the Irish political system. The ideal is not exclusive to Sinn Féin, as it is shared by most other Irish political parties (excluding Unionist parties obviously). What makes the difference, however, between these parties' stance and Sinn Féin's, is the place that Irish unity holds in their policy proposals and strategies.

While the party's commitment to Irish unity is beyond doubt, the manner in which the electorate appraises the merits of such an aspiration has many layers. To what extent do Irish voters choose an all-Ireland party when they cast their vote? Do they prioritise the left-wing vision of the party or do they buy into the rhetoric of Irish unity? Conversely, in Northern Ireland, while the debate has more salience, especially since Brexit, there are nuances in the approaches to this issue. Some measurement still uses what could be deemed a 'sectarian headcount', which categorises demographics according to religious affiliation, although the link between Nationalists and Irish unity might be less obvious than it would seem.

Undoubtedly the debate on Irish unity will take more prominence if Sinn Féin manages to sustain its February 2020 support base in the Republic of Ireland. However, some issues arise that are inevitably linked with its all-Ireland approach. Can the party deliver on social policies within a divided jurisdiction? It says it can and has the figures to prove it, but it also states that nothing is completely achievable within the present set-up. How it sells that contradiction to its electorate needs to be tested. Moreover, the fact that Sinn Féin is an all-Ireland party raises issues that no other party has to address: can it continue to be two different entities, one that needs to compromise in Northern Ireland as part of a coalition government, and one that can fully develop its left-wing rhetoric while in opposition in the Republic?

Whether the party likes it or not, the shadow of the IRA lingers on. However, the recurring debate over the IRA still being in a position to 'pull the strings' of the organisation is somehow rhetorical. Not that it is not fundamental, on the contrary. But there is no definite answer to this, much the same as regarding the question that hung over Gerry Adams' head for years about his alleged role as Chief of Staff in the IRA. While positions on this issue are entrenched – casting a shadow over the operation of Sinn Féin as a political party – this can also be a shortcut for some to justify their refusal to share power with them, by questioning the party's engagement with democratic processes and its suitability as a prospective government partner. Undoubtedly, this question stirs up a debate which has been ongoing on both sides of the border about the legacy of the conflict, the reassessment of the role that the IRA, and therefore Sinn Féin, played in it, and the manner in which this legacy can be overcome, or not, by all involved. Every new revelation concerning the IRA brings new challenges, new debates and new questions. However, the extent to which, with time, memory still determines electoral results and outcomes is central to understanding the present-day Sinn Féin. And while the former association with the IRA raises fundamental, soul-searching dilemmas for the party, and tests its capacity to shed its own past without repudiating it, it does not necessarily damage its image. It is these questionings and meanderings that this book seeks to unravel.

The United Ireland party

> We're Irish republicans. We're passionate about Irish unity,
> it's what we get up in the morning to try and achieve.
> (Pearse Doherty, YouTube, 05/07/20)

In 2018, when asked what the Good Friday Agreement
(GFA) fundamentally meant, Gerry Adams gave a puzzling
assessment: in his view, it 'doesn't pretend to be a settle-
ment. It is an agreement on a journey, without agreement
on the destination' (Adams, YouTube, 10/04/18). For
anyone with any knowledge about Sinn Féin, however,
this destination was very clear: the unification of Ireland,
which is what has driven, and justified, the party's existence. This makes Sinn Féin a unique political organisation within Ireland, one that has a vision to which it has
held steadfastly, one that can look beyond the ordinary
mandate and present a utopian project. Furthermore,
no other party is fully organised on both sides of the
island, with the exception of small, fringe organisations
that had not, as of the early 2020s, made any significant
breakthrough into the Irish political scene. Sinn Féin is

determined to provide a roadmap for the long-term future of the island. Reshaping the economy, remodelling society, and redressing inequalities, are all intertwined in the process that the party and its followers embarked upon a century ago and that, in spite of many setbacks and divisions, is still seen as the top priority.

Irish unity: a fundamental ideal, a fluctuating strategy

Dublin-based journalist Arthur Griffith would probably fail to recognise the current party as the latest incarnation of the movement known as Sinn Féin, which he founded in 1905. The main ingredient it has retained is also one of its most symbolic, and radical, strategies: abstentionism, which is still in place for Westminster elections, and in practice means that no elected Members of Parliament will take their seats in the House of Commons. The historical ties have thus not been entirely severed, as the logic that applied to this tactic in the early twentieth century is still considered valid today: that of refusing to recognise the authority of the UK, then the British Empire, over Ireland. Of course, historical and political conditions changed considerably throughout the twentieth century. Sinn Féin adapted its demands to the context in which it was operating, shifting its focus from the quest for self-determination until 1921, to the removal of the oath of allegiance[1] until the early 1930s, and then to the reunification of the island. Throughout this journey, it has retained its appetite for radicalism, rooted in the vision of a unified and independent Irish nation.

Territory has played an important role in the traditional framing of the Irish nation, being the central rationale for the claim to independence. Insularity further justified the belief that Ireland as a whole constituted a natural, self-contained unit. Indeed, one of the 1918 electoral manifestos for independence read: 'Look at the map! God had made Ireland Separate!' (Sinn Féin, n.d.). The unity of the territory has thus been at the heart of Sinn Féin's preoccupations. However, while this core principle has always been seen as non-negotiable, the party has shown it can be flexible when it comes to the strategies needed to achieve the goal. Gerry Kelly, long-term member of the Sinn Féin Ard Comhairle (Party Executive) and Member of the Local Assembly (MLA) explained: 'Irish republicans are highly respected around the world – especially in conflict zones – because of our versatility and ability to strategise and adapt to changing circumstances while keeping focused on our primary objective of uniting Ireland' (AP, 11/11/12). This adaptability was already visible when the Sinn Féin delegates accepted to sign the 1921 Treaty, which set in motion the process of autonomy for both sides of the island and therefore cemented partition. While this was seen by the anti-Treaty faction as a betrayal of the spirit and *raison d'être* of the party, it also showed a capacity to generate leaders who are willing, when at a crossroads, to override principles. The fact that those leaders were ultimately forced out of the party and created their own movements was Sinn Féin's major Achilles' heel, as it has shown a propensity for splits which can, momentarily at least, weaken the organisation. Thus, when Éamon De Valera, who was closely identified with the fight against the 1921 Treaty, decided in 1926 to lead his supporters into the Dáil – in spite of the strong opposition within Republican circles to the oath of allegiance that elected representatives had to swear to the British monarch – the only honourable, or pragmatic, course of action was for him to leave the party and form a new one, Fianna Fáil. Those who held on to the identity of Sinn Féin claimed the higher political moral ground, feeling that they were the true heirs of republicanism as embodied by the 1916 Proclamation. But they were also fighting a rear-guard battle which crippled their ability to adapt to changing circumstances. Despite its resilience, the party gradually sank into a state of quasi oblivion after De Valera's departure and that of a sizeable number of Sinn Féin delegates. Not even the most radical republicans were able to support the moribund party, which became estranged from all other kindred organisations such as Saor Eire,[2] Republican Congress[3] and even the IRA.[4] So while it might have seemed paramount to uphold principles, rigidity was what alienated Sinn Féin from its natural allies and drove it to a state of utter isolation and vulnerability.

The quest for a reunification of Ireland started in the mid-1920s, when the Border Commission finalised the partition of the island and copper-fastened a situation that had existed since the Treaty. Pro-Treaty IRA leader Michael Collins' vision of a secession that would ultimately prove unworkable (Rankin, 2006, 9) was buried with the confirmation of the boundaries that separated the six north-eastern counties from the rest of the island. Northern Ireland became a 'statelet', an autonomous province within the UK. More importantly, this new reality was seen as permanent by the Unionists who had sought to secede from the rest of the island and to remain within the British Empire. On the other hand, most parties in the newly established Free State concentrated on achieving economic and political stability and reinforcing the new institutions' sovereignty. The agenda of reunification, if embedded in their political core identity, was not a priority, nor was it acted upon (Coakley, 2017). With the 1937 constitution, the State, now Éire, reaffirmed its commitment to reunification, but was content with making this an aspiration rather than a priority, further binding the traditional narrative with 'the nation of Ireland being defined in terms of the island of Ireland' (Hayward, 2004, 23). For the decades to come, the national question would remain 'unfinished business' (Meagher, 2016).

While it could be argued that, until the early 1930s, Sinn Féin was more preoccupied in seeing the oath of allegiance removed than the reunification of the island, the border gradually became a more salient issue for Republicans, who were committed to using all means necessary to obtain its abolition. In the early 1930s, Sinn Féin put forward a vision of reunification strongly grounded in a 'Christian' ethos, which was more equated with Catholicism than with Protestantism. At the end of the same decade, the IRA embarked on an ill-fated military campaign in Ireland, or Plan S (for Sabotage), which sought the departure of the British from Northern Ireland.

However, little time was spent in analysing the reasons why this border existed in the first place or the resistance that unification would encounter. Instead, the British State was ascribed the entire responsibility for artificially designing those borders, with little, if any, consideration paid to the Unionists and to their fears, which were not openly acknowledged. Politically speaking, Unionism was seen as a by-product of British imperialism, which would lose its main rationale once the link with the rest of the UK was severed.

What revitalised the party in the late 1940s–early 1950s was its capacity to articulate an agenda centred, far more than in previous years, on the reunification of the island. Sinn Féin threw its weight behind the IRA's Border Campaign (1956–1962), nominating candidates to by-elections, which succeeded in putting its name on the Irish political map, as four of its candidates were elected to the Dáil in 1957. The new leadership thus managed to veer the party from the status of onlooker and guardian of principles to proponent of reunification, with a discourse increasingly anchored on Northern Ireland. It developed a vision as to the rationale and the running of a United Ireland, but didn't ignite 'national sentiment in a way that would transform the status quo' (Ferriter, 2019, 62). Ultimately, the failure of the armed campaign led to a radical change of direction, one that would eventually drive Sinn Féin to its most traumatic split since the foundation of Fianna Fáil. The 1969–1970 division between Provisionals and Officials, both within Sinn Féin and the IRA, left two factions that confronted

each other not so much on the principle of reunification, but on the best strategy to achieve it. Indeed, the
then leadership had begun to elaborate a more socialist,
Marxist view of how the new Ireland that it strived to
bring about would operate. In its view, this would be an
Ireland of workers and farmers. Although similar proposals had already been developed in the 1930s, these had
not been endorsed by Sinn Féin and the Second Dáil,[5]
who found them too radical, too left-wing. But with the
start of the civil rights movement, which was seeking the
introduction of reforms within the Northern Irish State,
Sinn Féin adapted its strategy to prioritise the unity of the
working class within Northern Ireland, as in its analysis
this would pave the way for a United Ireland. Therefore,
what common ground might have existed between the
Protestant and Catholic working classes was to be further
explored and built upon. However, whether this would
have been enough to overcome the fundamental division that separated the two communities is more open to
question. Provisional Sinn Féin was quite clear that this
would not be the case, as it considered a unification of the
working classes impossible while the Northern State was
in existence. They thus prioritised achieving the unity of
the island over the unity of the proletariat.

The 1969–1970 split saw the emergence of a highly
principled organisation, which believed in the tactics of
revolutionary warfare, opposing those who sought an alliance of the working classes in order to overthrow the
Unionist regime and undermine the British stronghold
on Northern Ireland. Ultimately, it is the rejection of

the very idea of reform that sustained the Provisionals' struggle throughout the conflict and that coloured their strategies in terms of how to reach their ultimate goal: a United Ireland.

Within a year of having been founded, Provisional Sinn Féin had developed a roadmap, *Éire Nua*, which was the closest the party came to a political programme. First published in 1971, it was the brainchild of the thinkers of the Provisional Movement, such as Ruairí and Seán Ó Brádaigh or Dáithí Ó Conaill. Somewhere in between the 1916 Declaration of 'the right of the people of Ireland to the ownership of Ireland' and a Marxist analysis, it advocated for public control of the means of production, the Nationalisation of banks and key industries as well as the ban on foreigners acquiring land in the country. *Éire Nua* had a two-pronged objective: to convince Unionism of the benefits of reunification, and to promote a vision that was grounded on what were deemed to be concrete and feasible proposals, within the overall objective of achieving a 32-county socialist republic. The socialism of the proposition stood for a mix of ideals: those of 1916, still seen as defining the ultimate vision of the future of Ireland; a genuine belief that workers should be prioritised in the process; and some more concrete proposals such as cooperatives and further worker involvement in the economy. More prominent in the documents was the attention paid to the Unionist/Protestant population, as it acknowledged their opposition in principle to a United Ireland. Based on the key organisational principle of federalism, *Éire Nua* was meant to address this opposition as

well as to allay fears. It divided Ireland into its four historical provinces, so as to ensure that each local/regional
community had an equal say. Ulster was to become
once again a nine-county province, which presented the
double advantage of breaking away from the partition
as originally designed, in Sinn Féin's eyes, by Britain
and Unionists, and restoring some demographic balance
between Catholics and Protestants within the North.
This was meant to dispel the Protestants' anxiety of being
immersed into a Catholic Ireland: while they would not
retain the straightforward majority that they held within
a six-county Northern Ireland, they would still remain
numerically strong and therefore in a position to defend
their interests. Paraphrasing Lord Craigavon's famous
1934 speech where he spoke of a 'Protestant parliament
and a Protestant people',[6] *Éire Nua* put forward the idea
of an 'Ulster Parliament for the Ulster people' and developed specific proposals outlining the rationale for the setting up of such parliaments (Sinn Féin, 1971).

The Provisionals' proposals were elaborated in a context that was not conducive to a discussion on the merits
of a United Ireland. The Northern Ireland parliament,
Stormont, had been suspended by the British government
in March 1972, which took over the administration of
the region through Direct Rule from Westminster. The
British authorities then organised a Northern Ireland
Sovereignty referendum, held on 8 March 1973, asking
the electorate whether they wanted Northern Ireland to
remain part of the UK or to be joined with the Republic of
Ireland outside the UK. Sinn Féin reacted with contempt,

seeing this consultation as a stratagem from the British to artificially boost their legitimacy in the region. Republicans claimed, as they had always done, that the only valid poll ever to be held was the general election of 1918, as it included the whole of Ireland. Sinn Féin therefore called upon its supporters to boycott the process, and the Social Democratic Labour Party (SDLP) followed suit on the basis that it was an 'irresponsible decision' by the British government as the party feared it would lead to an escalation of violence as a highly predictable outcome. Consequently, the results were not very telling, with 98.90% of the votes cast favouring retaining the union, while 41.34% of the electorate had followed the Nationalist/republican parties' call for a boycott and stayed away from the polling stations. In real terms, 57% of the electorate had chosen to remain within the UK (BBC, 09/03/73).

The issue of reunification remained at the top of Sinn Féin's agenda throughout the 1970s, with the publication of a number of pamphlets that complemented the federal project. However, with the advent of a new leadership and a radical change in strategies, *Éire Nua* fell out of favour. Whether it was ever held in any esteem by the younger generation of Northern Republicans who would eventually take over the leadership of Sinn Féin in the early 1980s is questionable, as the swift change of policy that followed the election of the new leadership would tend to demonstrate. In 1982, the Sinn Féin Ard Fheis deleted all references to the federal project from the party's constitution, as it was now seen as being counterproductive, a 'sop to Unionism'. Interestingly, *Éire Nua* had aroused the interest of some in Loyalist circles, and a tentative dialogue had taken place in the 1970s. But both mainstream Unionism and Nationalism failed to engage with the proposals, and Republicans went back to the drawing board on the issue of reunification. However, as the 1980–1981 hunger strikes had demonstrated, it would be next to impossible to achieve meaningful progress by force of arms only. Politics became a buzzword, and shorter-term objectives were set. With the adoption of the 'Armalite and ballot box' strategy[7] in 1981, which led Sinn Féin to play a more active role in the political arena, it was essential to put forward policy programmes that not only dealt with a hypothetical future, but that tackled concrete day-to-day issues. For the first time since the early 1920s, Sinn Féin was actually putting together a proper political programme. A United Ireland was still the core demand, but it was assorted with many other shorter-term objectives.

Sinn Féin soon reaped the benefits of its newly found electoral enthusiasm, securing an average of 10% of the vote in the Northern Ireland Assembly (1982), Westminster (1983) and European (1984) elections. But its performance in the Republic was still insignificant, and reunification was dependent on the party's ability to secure support on both sides of the border. This led Sinn Féin to question its strategy and to drop the abstentionist policy in the Dáil in 1985, a core principle according to which, until then, elected representatives did not take their seats in parliaments on either side of the border or in

Westminster. Such a move was made possible by the IRA giving its green light to the change, through a decision taken at its convention prior to the Sinn Féin Ard Fheis (*AP*, 14/10/14). The fact that for the first time since 1970, the military organisation held such a high-risk gathering given the security situation was in itself indicative of the importance of the issue. The IRA was thus demonstrating that it was capable of pragmatism and that principles were only valid as long as they served a purpose. But by accepting to sit in the Republic's national Assembly, Sinn Féin was not just making a pragmatic choice. It was acknowledging a change of direction. A United Ireland was still the priority, but its possible implementation was revised and was now inscribed in a long-term future. What needed to be done first was to win the hearts and minds of the voters on a number of more prosaic issues before selling them the reunification project. However, Sinn Féin was still criticised for its dogmatic and rigid position on reunification. 'Solutions to the problems of division in Ireland have been postponed by Nationalist/Republican concentration on the language of ideological rectitude rather than trying to face the political reality' (27/10/88), wrote a columnist in the *Irish Times*. On the left, many saw the very existence of the IRA as the main obstacle to reunification. The Labour and trade unionist movement thus urged Sinn Féin to support a 'joint campaign with activists in the British Labour Party. The IRA's terrorist campaign is a major obstacle to Irish unity. The political strategy of socialists and trade unionists should be aimed at isolating the armed struggle' (*IT*, 08/05/89).

Reunification and the peace process

The ideal of a United Ireland remained at the heart of the peace process as far as Sinn Féin was concerned. Its analysis clearly laid the responsibility for this happening onto the British. Republicans seemed convinced that the 'wish of the majority of British people themselves [is] that their government should withdraw from Ireland and Irish affairs' (*AP*, 21/05/97), a view that was not then supported by opinion polls.[8] Irish unity was posited as the key element to any successful future peace process. According to Adams, 'the British government's failure to commit themselves to a positive policy of working towards Irish reunification inevitably increases suspicions among Irish nationalists about Britain's real intentions' (*IT*, 21/05/97). Republicans went further, posing as a pre-condition to their participation in negotiations that the British government should play 'a crucial and constructive role in persuading Unionists to reach a democratic agreement on the issue of Irish national reunification with the rest of the people of this island and to encourage, facilitate and enable such agreement' (*IT*, 07/08/97).

The signing of the GFA in 1998 was a turning point in Sinn Féin's rhetoric on a United Ireland. Martin McGuinness, who alongside Adams had been championing the peace process and the political direction taken by the party, remained cautious in his appraisal of the new deal. A few days after the historic event, he claimed to be still unclear as to 'whether or not there is enough in the constitutional stuff to move us forward, in a transitional way, to our primary objective which is still and which always will be the eventual reunification of Ireland' (*AP*, 13/04/98). But once Sinn Féin decided to put all its weight behind the Agreement, it sold it to its supporters as a stepping stone, a blueprint for reunification. In order to convince their members that the goal remained unchanged, Republicans stressed the importance of the all-Ireland dimension of the institutions and pointed to the clause of the Agreement which enabled a referendum to be triggered. Interestingly, this constituted one of the main arguments used by both sides in the May 1998 referendum campaign. A study showed that the phrase 'United Ireland' in the Democratic Unionist Party (DUP) campaign leaflets 'usually appeared in bigger, bolder lettering than the surrounding text' and was meant as a deterrent for the electorate, predicting that the Agreement was a 'staging post' or 'would lead to' this outcome (Somerville & Kirby, 2012, 249). Nationalists for their part were divided between those who didn't necessarily want Irish unity in the short term, but saw the Agreement as an 'important political milestone in its own right, while republicans perceived it as a mere stepping stone to their ultimate goal of Irish unity' (Hayes & McAllister, 2001, 81). The manner in which Republicans spun this argument was the outcome of a careful and well-balanced rhetoric which combined traditional views on reunification and a newly acquired pragmatism at which leaders excelled throughout the peace process and that also enabled the party to overtake the SDLP as the main representative of the Nationalist community.[9]

The enthusiasm that Sinn Féin has displayed for the Northern Ireland institutions, notwithstanding a number of setbacks which have translated into repeated suspensions of the Executive, has been the subject of harsh criticism from opponents within its own camp (see McGlinchey, 2019). Indeed, in their view, the institutions created by the GFA are but a continuation of the partitionist structures which have characterised the history of Northern Ireland. However, Sinn Féin sees them as transitional, and while they are not the party's preferred option, they correspond to what the electorate clearly favours. Opinion polls indicate that out of all possible constitutional choices for Northern Ireland, the continued local representation is the arrangement that most respondents favour. The Northern Ireland Life and Times Survey (NILT), which takes place every year, has been asking the same question since 2007, and therefore provides a clear picture of what respondents believe the long-term status of Northern Ireland should be (see Figure 1).

The local Assembly option is thus, markedly, the preferred choice. The decline observed over the years 2016–2019 corresponds to the suspension of the institutions and to a possible disillusionment on the part of the electorate. However, this does not benefit either the Direct Rule or the United Ireland options, which variation in terms of people's preference only ebb slightly. On the other hand, the proportion of those who don't know has increased almost constantly. This raises a fundamental question for the party, as the successful operation of

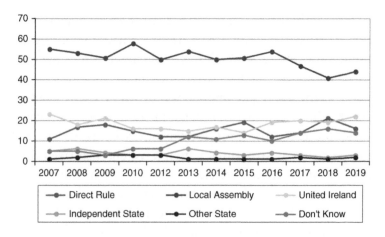

Figure 1 Constitutional preferences, 2007–2019

Source: Northern Ireland Life and Times Survey.

such institutions could be construed as a vindication of those who believe that Northern Ireland is a viable political entity, and that its continued presence within the UK is a workable solution. Obviously, it is a conundrum that Sinn Féin has to navigate, a contradiction that the party needs to manage. Caoimhe Archibald, Sinn Féin MLA for East Derry, believes that

> the institutions are very much valued in the North and we heard that over the three years they were down [2017–2020] [...] But we have to make sure they work properly. When we put that in the context of the debate around Irish unity, I think we have to be open to the type of arrangement that is going to be appealing to people, open to have the conversation about some sort of regional set-up as a transition. None of these things can be ruled out. People want to have their elected representatives, and it's a big jump to go from

what we have now to being represented in Leinster House. (Archibald, interview, October 2020).

However, Sinn Féin succeeded in turning this apparent contradiction into an argument which supports the work that public representatives carry out on behalf of their constituents, according to Archibald:

There isn't a contradiction between being in the institutions and arguing for a United Ireland, because the institutions and the GFA are based on the principle of con-sent which was designed to accommodate opposing views around constitutional issues. I think it's a matter of how this is managed. I would rather see strong good working institutions and good working relationships. (Archibald, interview, October 2020).

The prospect of a local Assembly within a United Ireland might ring a bell to those who advocated the fed-eral solution in the 1970s. What is different this time is that Sinn Féin is counting on its work with other political parties within the institutions to facilitate the discussion around the future operation of Northern Ireland within a united jurisdiction. Such an approach could not have been considered prior to the peace process. By making all parties work together, the GFA has at least created the conditions of a conversation. Sinn Féin is not now – any more than it was during the conflict – in a position to impose a solution, but it can use the official role that it now plays within the Assembly and the Executive to advocate for a concerted United Ireland. The party rejects the bleaker prospect of a violent backlash in the event of a reunification, believing that such fears are being artificially heightened by those who fiercely oppose this objective. In this logic, given that the process will be based on the consent of the majority, this scenario can and will be avoided.

Sinn Féin's all-Ireland competitors

Former Fianna Fáil Taoiseach Bertie Ahern once stated that the 1916 legacy needed to be reclaimed as it had been appropriated by the IRA and Sinn Féin.[10] To some extent, this could also be said of the objective of reunification, which for decades was closely associated with Sinn Féin's agenda, but which has been reintegrated within the discourse of most Irish political parties since the start of the twenty-first century. Undoubtedly, from the outset, both Fianna Fáil's and Fine Gael's stated aim has been to unite both parts of the island, and this is enshrined in their respective constitutions. Fianna Fáil seeks 'to secure in peace and agreement the unity of Ireland and its people' and Fine Gael's constitution opens with the statement that 'The name of the Party shall be Fine Gael (United Ireland)' (Fine Gael, 2014, 2). However, this did not necessarily translate into concrete actions or strategies. Until the 1960s, the Irish State 'prioritised the achievement of national unity in the 26 counties over territorial unity with a more diverse polity' (O'Malley & McGraw, 2017, 18). While Fianna Fáil leader Seán Lemass put together a Northern Ireland policy in the 1960s and Charles Haughey brought a stronger shade of Nationalism in the 1980s, neither of the two main parties actively campaigned for a United Ireland, both seeing this as a process that needed to be built on consent, thus making the ideal of reunification an aspiration more than a policy (Puirséil, 2017). The prospect of Irish unity did not, until recently, feature highly in either party's election manifestos.[11] Talk of a United Ireland, however, has undeniably accelerated since the June 2016 Brexit referendum. For instance, Fianna Fáil's leader, Micheál Martin, promised in 2017 a 12-point roadmap for the reunification of Ireland. Two years later, the plan had not yet materialised, and Martin explained to *The Journal* that this was a complex process that could not be rushed, which distinguished his party's approach to that of Sinn Féin, presented as too hasty and unsafe.

Until recently, Sinn Féin was the only major party organised on both sides of the border, thus having a lead on other parties on the issue of reunification. However, in 2007, and for the first time in its history, Fianna Fáil decided to explore the possibilities of venturing north of the border and getting involved in party politics, by building a partnership with an existing champion of the cause of reunification, the SDLP. Seen by many as the main architect behind the GFA, the Nationalist party founded at the start of the Troubles by John Hume paid a high price, in terms of electoral support, for its full involvement in the peace process. The explanations for this are varied, ranging from the so-called 'ethnic outbidding' seen as intrinsic to the GFA institutions which enabled Sinn Féin to present itself as the 'greener' of the two parties, to the loss of historical figures such as John Hume and Seamus Mallon, and a less efficient political machine (McGlinchey, 2019). Competing within the same electoral constituency, Sinn Féin has successfully presented itself as the more staunchly Nationalist of the two parties whilst simultaneously moderating its message and becoming incorporated into the institutions of Northern Ireland. As a former SDLP director of communications, Conal McDevitt, put it, 'The party "with no guns" to quote Tony Blair, was served up to Sinn Féin as the prize if they cooperated' (*Fortnight*, May 2008).

In 2020, two other parties were in direct competition with Sinn Féin, nominating candidates on both sides of the border. The first was the People Before Profit Alliance,[12] whose rhetoric on reunification is reminiscent of that used by Sinn Féin in the 1970s, with the ultimate goal being the establishment of a '32-county socialist republic'. However, they have yet to pose a serious challenge to Sinn Féin's hegemony in Northern Irish working-class, Nationalist strongholds. With 1.8% of the first preference votes in the 2017 Westminster general election (BBC, 2017), a figure which fell to 0.9% in the 2019 election, they hardly represent a dent in Sinn Féin's support, although their presence locally can be a challenge to Republican candidates, as was the case in 2017 when their candidate was ahead in the Northern Ireland Assembly election in the West Belfast constituency. The other all-Ireland organisation is Aontú, which was formed when Sinn Féin TD[13] Peadar Tóibín left the party in protest at its pro-choice stance in the Repeal the Eighth referendum and founded a movement dedicated to 'Life, Unity and Economic Justice'.[14] Aontú's leader was elected in the 2020 general election and his party obtained 1.48% of the vote in the Republic, while its share of the vote in Northern Ireland remains low, at 1.2%, showing the significant road Aontú still needs to travel to represent a challenge to Sinn Féin.

Brexit: a game changer for Irish unity?[15]

In a letter to the *New Statesman*, political scientist John Bew remarked in 2014: 'The Irish state has never been less interested in Irish reunification. The last thing that anyone in Dublin wants is any destabilisation of the status quo in Northern Ireland' (*New Statesman*, 28/02/14). Yet two years later, in September 2016, Taoiseach Enda Kenny talked of the 'possibility of unity by consent [which] must be maintained as a valid democratic option into the future' (*IT*, 09/09/16). In the interval between those two assessments, Brexit had taken place and the debates that it generated were holding centre stage.

On 16 June 2016, the UK electorate was asked to decide whether to remain in the European Union or to leave. The campaign had been dominated by issues of immigration and national identity (Virdee & McGeever, 2018), leaving the elephant in the room hardly mentioned: what would happen to the border between the two sides of Ireland if they were no longer part of the same supranational jurisdiction? What would become of the GFA, which was heavily predicated upon both signatories being member states of the EU? Warnings of the potentially disastrous consequences for Northern Ireland of a Yes vote had been voiced. Former Prime Ministers John Major and Tony Blair made a joint appeal in Derry to the Northern Irish electorate to choose to remain within the EU, highlighting the difficulties ahead if the Leave vote were to prevail (*Guardian*, 09/06/16). Taoiseach Enda Kenny also pleaded with UK voters and particularly with the Northern Irish business community to vote for Remain in order not to jeopardise the economic links and the trade which were deemed essential for both jurisdictions' economic well-being. However, these calls might not have been heard on the other side of the Irish Sea, or perhaps Northern Ireland was not seen by the electorate as a priority. Overall, the UK voted to leave the EU, with 51.9% in favour, while Northern Ireland, with a resounding 55.8% of the vote, chose to remain.[16]

The seeds of the post-Brexit debate had been sown in the campaign arguments which both sides developed in Northern Ireland. The only party which had sided with Brexiters was the DUP. Not only had it always been quite Eurosceptic, it shared the Brexiters' concerns on the issues of sovereignty, finances and, ultimately, it saw a UK outside of the EU as a way to cement all its different components and to reassert Northern Ireland's status as a full member of the Union. The red line was drawn at any outcome which would result in Northern Ireland being treated differently to any other part of the UK. The second largest Unionist formation, the UUP (Ulster Unionist Party), was divided on the issue, with its leader Mike Nesbitt advocating a Remain vote, warning that

'Northern Ireland will acutely feel the implications of a Brexit; constitutionally, financially and politically' (*Newsletter*, 21/06/16). However, given the divisions that emerged within the party, with some such as local councillor George Shiels believing that the EU was 'bleeding the UK dry', no formal voting instructions were issued. On the Nationalist side, both Sinn Féin and the SDLP campaigned for a Remain vote, for similar reasons. The SDLP's slogan, 'Brexit is bad for Britain, bad for Europe, bad for Ireland and a disaster for Northern Ireland' summed it all up. The EU was seen as having enabled the cementing of the peace process, providing funding and enhancing Anglo-Irish relations. Sinn Féin paid particular attention to the issue of the border and of North–South cooperation. Interestingly, Republicans have never been fully supportive of the EU. Although they have gone from being staunchly opposed to the European Economic Community in the 1970s and 1980s to developing a position of 'critical' engagement with the EU, they are still concerned at the perceived loss of sovereignty that membership entails. As Sinn Féin President Mary Lou McDonald noted in 2020, 'We're not arguing that the European project is perfect, far from it, we are profoundly critical of the economic model, of foreign policy, a whole rake of issues but whatever the issues are, a Tory Brexit was never the answer' (McDonald, YouTube, 05/07/20).[17] However, the party also realised from the start of the peace process how a supranational institution could be used to further the cause of Irish unity. In 2006, Mary Lou McDonald stated that 'the economic prospects for a United Ireland look very promising. Therefore, it is in the interest of the EU to do what it can to encourage this development and to act as advocates for Irish unity' (PR, 10/05/06). Successive Irish governments, for their part, saw the EU as making the question of unity less pressing since there is the impression that 'internal territorial borders are de facto no longer significant' (Hayward, n.d., 24), but Brexit highlighted the many difficulties, contradictions and apparently unsolvable positions that the issue of the border created for the Republic of Ireland, for the UK, and ultimately for the EU itself.

However, throughout most of the process of negotiating a deal between the UK and the EU, Sinn Féin had no official platform from which to make its case heard. Indeed, the Northern Irish institutions were suspended a mere six months after the referendum. This had nothing to do with Brexit, but was precipitated by the 'Cash for Ash' controversy, a plan designed to incentivise renewable energy, but that ended up costing the Northern Ireland Exchequer more than £500 million.[18] Sinn Féin Deputy First Minister Martin McGuinness had called on DUP leader Arlene Foster to resign while the matter was being investigated, believing that the 'credibility of the political institutions [was] being undermined', to which the First Minister had retorted that she did not take her lead from Sinn Féin (BBC, 16/12/16). Mc Guinness resigned in January 2017, effectively putting an end to ten years of devolved government, the longest period that the Northern Ireland Executive had been in session since the forming of the institutions. Interestingly, however, one of the major rifts between Sinn Fein and the DUP, one that would derail negotiations on the restoration of the institutions, was not about Brexit or about constitutional issues, but centred on the Irish language which became 'something of a proxy war' between the two parties throughout 2017 (Fenton, 2018, 146). Sinn Fein insisted on the necessity of introducing a standalone Irish Language Act, which would put the Irish language on a par with English, and thus redress decades of neglect of the Irish cultural identity and tradition. Unionists, on the other hand, felt that this was a tool being used by Sinn Féin to further promote a United Ireland and feared that this would threaten their own identity.[19]

The situation generated by the collapse of the institutions was compounded by the June 2017 British general election, which further entrenched divisions. The SDLP lost its three seats to Sinn Féin who won seven. Moreover, with 326 out of 650 seats, the Conservative Party had to rely on the support of its 'friends and allies' from the DUP to compensate for its lack of overall majority. The 'Confidence and supply agreement' reassured Unionists as to the fact that no border poll would be held without the 'consent of the people', but it also damaged the UK's image as a neutral facilitator of the GFA. Indeed, reactions to this alliance were cool, to say the least. Irish Taoiseach Enda Kenny stated that such a deal could put the peace process at risk. The British conservatives were seen as taking sides, no matter what the costs were. Sinn Féin was, predictably, even more scathing of the deal which it saw as a betrayal by the DUP of the interests of

Northern Ireland, exposing Conservatives' 'increasingly partisan approach' to Northern Ireland' (*IE*, 10/06/17).

Brexit certainly changed the political landscape in Northern Ireland on many different levels. The EU had 'acted as a unique catalyst for bilateral discussions between the UK and Irish governments' (Hayward & Murphy, 2018, 278). The debates that followed the referendum inevitably impacted intergovernmental relations. The peace process was underpinned by a steady and healthy relationship between the UK and the Republic of Ireland, who as co-facilitators would speak in unison, but the nature of that relationship was put to the test throughout the Brexit negotiations and was, to some extent, strained. The Irish government came under fire and was heavily criticised by Conservative and Unionist politicians. Robin Swann, then leader of the UUP, made no secret of his disapproval, on an occasion which was in itself quite remarkable, as he was the first ever UUP leader invited to the Fine Gael Ard Fheis in 2018. Acknowledging that the relationship between both sides of the island, which had improved with the GFA, had experienced new tensions after the referendum, he added: 'When my party raised legitimate concerns over the backstop, that seemed to be met with a "suck it up" attitude' (BBC, 17/11/18). Unionists felt that the issues of the border and the peace process were used by Brexit opponents to thwart its implementation (BBC, 24/11/17).

Ironically, from 2017 to 2019, Sinn Féin was the only anti-Brexit party with a representation in Westminster. However, due to its continued observance of the abstentionist policy, none of its seven elected representatives took their seats. The party came under pressure at times to use its Westminster representation in order to contribute to the debate on Brexit and perhaps even to challenge the outcome of the vote. Such a case was made by *Irish Times* columnist Fintan O'Toole, who accused Sinn Féin of neglecting its responsibility and, worse still, of wishing for a 'crash' Brexit which would suit their objectives, as the crisis that such a scenario would generate could precipitate the debate on reunification. However, Mary Lou McDonald replied, in a column published by *An Phoblacht*, that O'Toole's argument was based on 'flawed mathematics and political wishful thinking' and further argued that shifting the blame onto Sinn Féin was not only inaccurate, but targeted the wrong culprits, who were obviously the hard-core Brexiters (*AP*, 07/09/19). McDonald made two noteworthy points. The first was to credit Sinn Féin with the idea of a backstop. This mechanism was devised to avoid the return of a hard border between the two sides of the island by keeping Northern Ireland within the customs union and avoiding controls at the border. According to McDonald, the origins of the proposal were to be found in the special designated status advocated by the party in April 2017, which called for the freedom of movement of goods, people and services,[20] and which 'found expression in the backstop'. RTE's EU Editor, for his part, traces the birth of the backstop, on 8 November 2017, to 'one bullet point of six at the bottom of a "working paper" circulated that morning by Michel Barnier's team' (Connolly, 2018).

The second point worthy of mention is the manner in which McDonald referred to abstentionism as representing an 'electoral mandate'. Indeed, those choosing to cast their vote for Sinn Féin in the Westminster elections do so in the knowledge that they will not be sending their representatives to the House of Commons. However, this strategy is no longer in place for any other parliamentary institutions, as it was dropped for the Dáil in 1985 and was never even considered for the Belfast Agreement institutions. Thus abstentionism from Westminster could be seen as a remnant of a radical past when Republicans did not engage with the locus of power, preferring to keep to the side-lines, but maintaining their opposition by other means. As Michelle Guildernew, Sinn Féin MP for Fermanagh South Tyrone, noted, 'Irish interests never have and never will be served in a British parliament' (*IT*, 11/11/19). However, Sinn Féin can also make pragmatic choices, as was the case when the party decided not to nominate candidates in three of the 18 Northern constituencies for the 2019 general election in order to ensure the election of a Remain candidate. In practice, this meant urging its electorate to vote for an independent, an Alliance and a SDLP candidate. However, by doing so, the party ran the risk of sending a contradictory message. Indeed, if representation at Westminster is not seen as a useful tool to advance its agenda, why help the election of a candidate who will take their seat? Beyond the anti-Brexit agenda, which led the SDLP to replicate the tactic by not fielding candidates in three constituencies, this move could be seen as an attempt to placate those among its Northern voters who no longer steadfastly believe in the abstentionist strategy. Indeed, while some, such as North Belfast candidate John Finucane described his stance as 'proudly abstentionist', a survey published in the *Belfast Telegraph* in January 2020 showed that a growing number of the party's electorate was in favour of dropping this stance, with 20.6% in favour as opposed to only 1.6% in 2017 (*BT*, 10/01/20).

'Unstoppable conversation'

Sinn Féin seized the opportunity that was generated by the topic of the Irish border within the greater Brexit debate to demand the holding of a poll. The GFA outlined in vague terms a strategy to proceed to the unification of the Irish territory, if this was to ever happen. It gave the Secretary of State for Northern Ireland the power to organise a border poll 'if at any time it appears likely to him that a majority of those voting would express a wish that Northern Ireland should cease to be part of the United Kingdom and form part of a united Ireland' (GFA, 1998, 5). However, this clause left a number of questions unanswered, such as the definition of the criteria for holding a poll, which according to the independent British think-tank Institute for Government is quite vague: 'a consistent majority in opinion polls, a Catholic majority in a census, a Nationalist majority in the Northern Ireland Assembly, or a vote by a majority in the Assembly' (Institute for Government, 2019). The clause does not spell out how the process of reunification could be implemented or what form it could take; nor does it outline what will happen if it is chosen by a close majority, or state whether both sides of the island must in conjunction agree to a reunification. Perhaps this lack of precision was deliberate as it contributed to making this clause acceptable to the Unionist community. The principle at the heart of this process, however, is clearly defined: consent. No reunification can be envisaged unless it is agreed by a majority of the population of Northern Ireland. If the outcome of a poll is negative, supporters of a United Ireland will have to wait for seven years before a new one can be called. Timing is thus of the essence. While the prospects for proponents of a United Ireland are open-ended, the stakes are much higher for its opponents, as a majority would determine their fate once and for all.

Brexit considerably shifted the general discussion on reunification in the Republic of Ireland. For Sinn Féin, it has contributed to raising awareness and making this aspiration into a more tangible matter. Mairéad Farrell, TD for West Galway, sees it as

> definitely an issue, it has become more of an issue for people in Galway over the last number of years. Before that, it just hadn't been something that was part of their daily reality, just because if you choose to ignore it, when you're living in Galway, you can, because your life is so far removed from it. But those two issues [Brexit and COVID-19] really brought it back to the forefront of people's minds'. (Farrell, interview, September 2020)

However, political parties maintain that the approach to the process of reunification must be cautious, in order not to antagonise the section of the population that is most opposed to this scenario, the Unionists. Most parties are dubious as to the merits of holding a border poll in the short-to-medium term and would concur with Labour leader Brendan Howlin's 2019 assessment: 'If any lessons are to be learned from Brexit it is that if we are to make any definitive constitutional decisions, an enormous amount of advance preparation needs to be done' (*DD*, 06/11/19). Fine Gael deems it risky to engage in such a venture unless there is certainty as to the outcome on both sides of the border. For Taoiseach Leo Varadkar:

> calls for Border polls, whether from Sinn Féin or People Before Profit, are really unhelpful at present. What we are trying to say to Unionists in Northern Ireland is that at the heart of the Good Friday Agreement is acceptance of the principle of consent, acceptance not only that Northern Ireland is part of the UK, but also that Northern Ireland is different and needs special arrangements on occasion. (*DD*, 21/11/18)

Fianna Fáil also felt that pressing for a border poll, particularly in the midst of delicate negotiations over Brexit and the border, was at best unhelpful, at worst counterproductive. According to TD Lisa Chamber 'Sinn Féin has continually called for a Border poll, which has only served to reverse the progress made in Northern Ireland and sow seeds of division and mistrust, which has prevented the parties from working together to restore the Executive and to achieve the best Brexit deal possible' (*DD*, 17/05/18).

On the other hand, Sinn Féin is pressing for a border poll to be held as soon as possible. As Sinn Féin TD David Cullinane put it, 'we have been screaming from the rooftops at successive Irish Governments for years to plan for Irish unity' *(DD*, 06/03/19). The party has, on a number of occasions, called on the British Secretary of State for Northern Ireland to organise the holding of a poll, without however making an argument that the authorities would consider compelling enough to accede to such a demand. It is notably on this issue that Sinn Féin has used most effectively its unique position of having a foot in both jurisdictions, by devising a strategy that addresses both the British and the Irish governments at the same time. In 2012 a group supporting reunification, United Ireland-You Decide, organised a mini-poll in the border communities of Creggan Upper (Louth, Republic of Ireland) and Crossmaglen (Armagh, Northern Ireland). The result was a foregone conclusion: 93.8% were in favour of a United Ireland. The validity of such results is questionable, as those who voted were most certainly already convinced of the benefits of this prospect, and the constituencies in which the poll took place were overwhelmingly Nationalist. But the objective was clearly attained as it gave those supporting the aim of a United Ireland a clear presence in the debate and ensured that this question remained visible. Sinn Féin described the poll as a 'very clear signal of strong demand' for a United Ireland *(IT*, 27/05/13). Strabane/Lifford followed suit and organised their own poll in the wake of the first mini-poll.

Sinn Féin has also been lobbying for the setting up of a Citizens' Assembly in the Republic (*The Journal*, 11/02/20). This model was used to prepare a nationwide consultation on a highly sensitive issue, the repeal of the Eighth Amendment of the constitution, which made the termination of a pregnancy unconstitutional in Ireland. This process followed the holding of the Irish Constitutional Convention which sat between 2012 and 2014. A total of 99 citizens were selected to take part in a consultation that looked at five different issues (ageing population, climate change, the holding of referenda, fixed-term parliaments and the Eighth Amendment). The question that both raised most interest and produced concrete outcomes was the latter, with 12,200 submissions and the holding of a referendum.[21] The Citizens' Assembly thus made it possible for the country as a whole to discuss the topic and ensured that the campaign would not be too polarising, enabling both sides to rehearse their arguments and to understand all the changes that an amendment of the constitution would imply. This process was seen as a tool providing the 'linking of deliberative democracy (mini-publics) and direct democracy (referendums)' (Farrell, Suiter & Harris, 2019). Having studied the submissions sent to the Assembly, a study concluded that the 'core arguments motivating these submissions continued to motivate voters', and in that respect, whether the outcome of the Assembly had been to inform voters or influence 'political narratives', it deemed the process significant (de Londras & Markicevic, 2018, 97). A debate that involves the entire population is what Republicans advocate. According to Sinn Féin TD Mairéad Farrell: 'the point is that we all take part in that conversation again. Something that we really saw in the last two referenda, people were just talking about the issue, with their own views and influences. It's not a Sinn Féin agenda. We want it to be much broader than that, get everyone involved' (Farrell, interview, September 2020).

The merit of holding a Citizens' Assembly on Irish unity was discussed in the Dáil in November 2019, after 1.088 members of civil society from both sides of the border sent an open letter to Leo Varadkar. The group, called *Ireland's Future*, led by Belfast solicitor Niall Murphy, claimed no political affiliation. It brought together signatories from various backgrounds (actors, singers, writers, academics).[22] Taoiseach Leo Varadkar did not rule out the prospect, but insisted that the timing needed to be right, as the government had already committed to other assemblies (on gender equality and biodiversity). Furthermore, it was feared that Unionists would decline to engage with the Assembly, making it a 'pan-Nationalist'[23] discussion and thus failing to include those most opposed to the prospect. Indeed, First Minister Arlene Foster indicated that her party would not participate 'in any all-Ireland civic forum because we believe in the Union' (*BT*, 29/11/19). In the *Irish Times*, commentator Stephen Collins saw such initiatives as an attempt to exploit Unionist anxieties, at their height during the time, given the uncertainties surrounding Brexit. His colleague Newton Emerson agreed with the importance of the time factor, but nevertheless pointed to the fact that Unionists could not be the sole deciders of the process, as their refusal to engage could be seen as a way to hold on to the so-called 'Unionist veto' (*IT*, 28/11/19).

UUP leader Steve Aiken is convinced that not only will Brexit not act as a catalyst for a United Ireland, but that the COVID-19 crisis has shown the Republic would never be in a position to afford Northern Ireland (Aiken, interview, April 2020). Sinn Féin's reasoning is the exact opposite: the objective of a United Ireland is within the reach of the present generation of leaders, whose responsibility it is to achieve it. The arguments put forward to support this view are multiple. Partition is still seen as the foundational cause of sectarianism, which can only be uprooted with reunification. The division of the island is also seen as a waste of resources which creates 'stagnating economic growth on both sides of the island, but particularly in the North'. McDonald thus talks of 'Two broken systems [and] a broken economic model' (Doherty, YouTube, 05/07/20). To the Unionist rebuke that the Republic will never be in a position to match the sums that the UK invests in Northern Ireland, and thus will never be able to afford reunification (Aiken, interview, April 2020), Doherty answers that the question is not 'can we afford Irish unity, the real question is, can we afford partition, and I believe we can't' (Doherty, YouTube, 05/07/20). Indeed, he notes that the figure of £9bn to £10bn which is often quoted as representing the subsidy (the gap between government spending and the amount raised in taxes) that the British Exchequer makes to the Northern Ireland budget every year is a myth, a 'mish-mash of local spending, accounting procedures, and billions of pounds of British obligations that simply wouldn't exist in the event of Irish unity' (Doherty, YouTube, 05/07/20). A study from the Irish Economic and Social Research Institute also concluded that the argument according to which the Irish State would need to take over the financial burden which is presently shouldered by the British Exchequer is 'questionable'. In the event of reunification, the existing subsidy would drop for a number of reasons: some of the current Northern Ireland expenditure would no longer be relevant (the 'non-identifiable expenditure' such as the contribution to the UK military force or debt servicing), amounting to 26% of the total subvention; moreover, the current levels reflect the low productivity of the Northern Ireland economy (McGuinness & Bergin, 2019). For some, the simple fact that the Northern economy is subsidised, no matter to what level, is in itself problematic: 'any state that, according to the British government figures, still requires a £10bn annual subvention 100 years after its creation cannot be considered a success or sustainable' (Gosling, 2018). The argument made by pro-unity campaigners is that the economy in the Republic could sustain the initial cost of reunification, which would only have positive outcomes in the medium term.

To further strengthen its argument, Sinn Féin has put together a number of policy documents that aim to demonstrate the economic benefits of reunification. Its 2018 *A United Ireland – Better for Jobs, Enterprise and Research* publication outlines the ways in which partition is detrimental to trade and businesses and puts forward detailed proposals that would enhance cooperation and trade, maximise tourism, attract Foreign Direct Investment and promote Irish products, produce and business. This would boost what is termed 'Brand Ireland'. The party has further fine-tuned its proposal with the elaboration of a document dedicated to the health services, for which they advocate the setting up of an all-Ireland National Health Service based on universal provision 'free at the point of delivery and funded through general taxation for all citizens across the entire island' (Sinn Féin, 2018a, 11). The COVID-19 crisis has reinforced their conviction that there is no sense in having two different jurisdictions when it comes to health. McDonald pointed out the absurdity of having a common policy for animals but not for humans, and Deputy First Minister Michelle O'Neill stated at the start of the pandemic that the virus knew no boundaries and therefore an all-Ireland coordinated effort was the only way to combat it effectively. This point was also developed by historian Diarmuid Ferriter in the *Irish Times*, when, assessing the North–South border approach to COVID-19, he concluded that 'there is insufficient uniformity which, given the size of the island, is absurd' (*IT*, 26/10/20).

Sinn Féin stops short of being triumphalist on the issue of reunification, being aware that some distance needs to be travelled before this can become a consensual prospect. Therefore, the target is not 'to make the Free State an enlarged 32 counties', as this would mean 'more of the same' and would perpetuate the broken system. Rather,

Sinn Féin's United Ireland will be, in their own words, a progressive society which would see the eradication of homelessness, the introduction of a universal health system, and the improvement of basic infrastructures. The main argument focuses on the economic waste that running two different health care systems, for instance, represents for the overall economy. It sees the priority, however, in mitigating the 'disastrous policies of what was really a squabble within the Tory party that is played out on the island of Ireland'. The party is convinced that Brexit has 'accelerated the discussion on Irish unity' and the approach taken by the British government can only confirm, in its view, that 'England's interest is never in relation to the North, it will always be an afterthought' (Doherty, YouTube, 05/07/20).

Unionist dilemma

Sinn Féin's optimism and confidence about the prospect of a United Ireland are matched by Unionism's adamant claim that this will simply not happen. They are reluctant to engage with any discussion led by the Republic, as they forecast that it would not be conducive to a fair and balanced process. They are unconvinced by the rhetoric deployed by official representatives such as Senator Mark Daly, who authored the first-ever report by the Oireachtas on a United Ireland: *Brexit & the Future of Ireland: Uniting Ireland & its People in Peace & Prosperity*. One of its key recommendations is that the 'Fears and concerns of the Unionist community need to be examined, understood and addressed comprehensively by all stake-holders in advance of any referendum'. UUP Steve Aiken, however, feels that the process is thwarted from the outset. 'Senator Daly wants me to be part of a conversation about me giving up my country, but he doesn't want to be part of the conversation about him giving up his. So where is the equivalence there? There is no reciprocity and there never has been' (Aiken, interview, April 2020). While the argument can seem convoluted, it does show that there are still fundamental concerns to be addressed, such as those identified by the few Unionists who contributed to the process in the 2019 follow-up report: loss of identity, triumphalism by Nationalists, retribution on former members of the RUC, British Army and Prison Officers, land being taken from Unionist farmers, return to violence, returning to the European Union after voting for Brexit, and healthcare, welfare and the economy (Daly, 2019). At times, the Unionist approach to a United Ireland verges on denial. But there is logic to its position. In their view, the GFA was acceptable because it reinforced the Union. Consequently, there is no point in engaging in debates on the end of the Union as it is protected by an international agreement.

The conundrum for Unionists is real. Their position is fragile, as was shown in the wake of the December 2019 Westminster general election, which saw the Conservative Party, with 365 seats and 43% of first preference vote, obtain an overall majority. The fact that newly elected Prime Minister Boris Johnson was prepared to sacrifice the Unionist demand for a ban on the backstop, still seen as an absolute red line, raised the question of the extent of the support for the Unionist cause in Conservative circles. The deal, which included a Northern Ireland Protocol, provided for Northern Ireland to remain *de jure* inside the UK Customs Territory, but *de facto* in the EU Customs Union, introducing some checks on certain goods coming from Great Britain (England, Scotland and Wales) and creating a regulatory and customs border in the Irish Sea. This led Jim Allister, leader of the radical Traditional Unionist Voice, a breakaway group from the DUP, to conclude that it 'puts [Northern Ireland] in a waiting room for Irish unity' (*PR*, 09/12/20). But the ongoing Brexit 'psychodrama', as one *Irish Times* commentator called it, regained momentum when the British government put forward an Internal Market Bill, giving ministers the power to simplify the paperwork necessary for products that transited from the EU to the UK via Northern Ireland. This bill, which its proponents presented as an 'insurance policy' that would further strengthen the Union, was seen by Irish and EU officials as a breach of an international treaty. The DUP felt somehow vindicated by this new twist in the Brexit debate, as Arlene Foster railed against the EU in Westminster that Northern Ireland was 'not the plaything of the EU' and thus could not be used 'to get their own way'. The final EU–UK deal, reached on 24 December 2020, reverted yet again to the British position on the backstop, albeit under a different guise. However, in view of the chaos predicted had the UK exited the EU without a deal, both DUP Arlene Foster and Sinn Féin Michelle O'Neill welcomed the deal. The DUP was criticised by its UUP rivals for accepting what it had claimed would not be acceptable: 'the DUP's blood red line about a border in the Irish Sea was never a red line at all', scoffed Steve Aiken, to which Arlene Foster retorted that while her party did not want the Protocol, it was there and it needed to be mitigated (BBC, 04/01/21).

It would thus seem that as steadfast in their opposition to the prospect of a United Ireland the Unionists remain, some pragmatism has emerged within their ranks. Indeed, not engaging at all with the overall conversation also represents a risk, even though the default position is still to deny that the possibility of reunification exists. Former DUP First Minister Peter Robinson suggested that Unionists should at least look at the issue, as a sort of 'insurance policy': 'I don't expect my own house to burn down, but I still insure it because it could happen' (IT, 28/07/18). The dilemma for Unionists is the following. On the one hand, they cannot envisage a situation where they might have to consider such a prospect, as UUP Reg Empey's angry reaction showed: 'Peter Robinson is playing into the hands of our country's opponents', seeing this type of declaration as an 'echo chamber for Sinn Féin' (IT, 28/07/18). On the other hand, they cannot totally stay out of the conversation, if only because they need their voice to be heard and to be proven right. A more nuanced approach came, unexpectedly perhaps, from some within the DUP. Gregory Campbell, for instance, explained that 'Many, many people take out insurance policies for issues that never come about. But you take it out for the possibility that it might. So that is a relevant point' (*IT*, 28/07/18). However, UUP's Steve Aiken rejects this type of talk: 'But why would we prepare for something that we don't expect is ever going to happen? Why would you create a poisonous debate about something that is not going to happen?' Robinson, however, reiterated two years later his opinion that denial was possibly the worst position that Unionism could take on the issue. In a letter to the *Newsletter*, a pro-Unionist daily publication, he wrote: 'I know there are border poll deniers who think such a referendum will never be called or believe that to talk about and prepare for a plebiscite creates momentum that will speed its arrival. I do not subscribe to such complacent and dangerous thinking'. He therefore suggested the formation of a pro-union think tank that would gather 'academics, professionals and additional specialists along with a small representative group of unionist influencers'. Robinson doesn't doubt that the 'case for the Union is compelling and logical', but he also warns of the dangers of not being prepared. 'It will depend as much on those who are pro-Union but do not vote for a party with unionist in its title and those who do not normally vote at all. It will depend on people from all backgrounds and minorities realising the Union is the best choice' (Robinson, *Newsletter*, 23/10/20).

Robinson's proposal came in the wake of the launch by Micheál Martin of the 'Shared Island' initiative which, as noted in an LSE blog, 'although rooted in different ideologies, both initiatives potentially mark a watershed in the development of nationalism and unionism on the island by ceasing to view the future through "the prism" of the past' (LSE blog 02/11/20). In his address, the Irish Taoiseach urged for a move away from bi-partisan identities, as 'the genius of the Agreement is that we do not need to be defined or dominated by constitutional questions, as we were in the past'. Martin's speech sought consensus and focused on cooperation between the two sides of the island, presented as a necessity to meet major strategic challenges, to develop the economy and to increase cooperation in areas such as health and education, and committed €500 million to initiatives supporting cross-border infrastructure projects (PR, 15/10/20).

A close analysis[24] of the language chosen by Martin reveals some overall trends: hardly any reference is made to Ireland, the actual term being only used alongside 'Northern'; rather, the more commonly found term is 'Island' (60 mentions). United or Unity are equally absent, the key adjective being 'shared' (40 mentions). Other important words include 'future' (19), 'agreement' (18), 'together' (14) (PR, 22/10/20). This careful selection of rhetorical tools undoubtedly meant to be as consensual as possible contrasts with the language used by Sinn Féin when discussing its all-Ireland agenda. A word frequency analysis of the short Sinn Féin document that introduces their website 'A decade of Opportunity – Towards the New Republic'[25] reveals that the most used terms were 'Irish' (13) and 'unity' (12), with 'referendum' coming in third place.

From shared Ireland to United Ireland?

Both Sinn Féin and Unionists do agree on one point: having public opinion on their side is key. Undoubtedly, the demographic trends that were revealed by the 2011 census open up different interpretations regarding the manner in which the population would vote in a border poll. Fast demographic changes are taking place in Northern Ireland, forecasting a reversal in the ratio of the Catholic/Protestant communities, which according to the 2011 census stood at 41% against 42% (Hayward & McManus, 2019, 141). Indeed, among the most salient demographic changes are an ageing Protestant community, as the highest percentages were to be found only in the older age group (60+) whereas the younger the demographic category was, the less likely they were to identify as Protestants. However, what has been termed the 'sectarian headcount' of Northern Irish demographics seems less and less relevant. The 2011 census provided an insight into the manner in which respondents identified: 40% saw themselves as British only, 25% as Irish only, 21% as Northern Irish only and 14% as other. A 2018 study looked at the 'neither' category in which the number of those who do not identify as either Unionist or Nationalist is fluctuating but rising, standing at 41% in 2017 (Hayward & McManus, 2019, 143). These findings were confirmed by a subsequent study in 2020, which concluded that it is possible to envisage a situation where the majority no longer identifies along binary lines (Cooley, 2020). Steve Aiken is convinced that demographics will not be a game changer per se. In his analysis, the 'neither' category is still broadly attached to the Union, therefore he does not see any merit in engaging with his southern counterparts on the issue of a United Ireland (Aiken, interview, April 2020).

Furthermore, constitutional preferences are also influenced by the political context, and the impact of Brexit cannot be overestimated. Indeed, faced with the prospect of a return to border controls, 'the Irish nationalist population has become more militant, and more monolithic' (Doyle & Connolly, 2019, 87). The polling institute Lucid Talk undertook a major survey which analysed opinion in light of different outcomes. In a 'no deal' scenario', a majority of 55% (48% '100% certain' and 7% 'probable') opted to join a United Ireland, while 42% (38% '100% certain' and 4% 'probable') chose to remain in the UK. However, the same question with a withdrawal agreement changed the ratio: those who were in favour of joining a United Ireland dropped to 38% (30% and 18%) with 48% against (39% and 9%). Finally, when presented with a scenario where the UK would remain in the EU, the ratio of those who wanted to join a United Ireland fell again to 29% (21% and 8%) and rose substantially to 60% for those wishing to remain in the UK (47% and 13%), although, interestingly, the ratio of those undecided also increased (from 4% to 11%) (Lucid Talk, 2018). The same organisation carried out a further survey in February 2020. Asked whether a border poll should be held, 36.1% were in favour, compared with 22.6% who were against, 'never at any time, now or in the future'. However, almost 40%

were hesitant ('Maybe – only at some stage in the future') and 1.8% didn't know. Perhaps the two constituencies that need to be most convinced on each side are the non-aligned voters and the young voters, who are the ones less likely than other groups to claim binary identities. The results were more promising for the pro-Unity campaign, with a majority of Alliance voters (47%) and 18–45 year olds (50%) opting for a United Ireland, as opposed to 22% and 46% choosing to remain part of the UK (Lucid Talk/ the detail, February 2020). One year later, in January 2021, Lucid Talk's survey results showed a substantial increase in the number of those who preferred a United Ireland (41.3% against 46.8 who opted to remain within the UK), with those unsure dropping to 10%. When surveying those who had voted for non-Nationalist or Unionist parties, the proportion of those favouring a United Ireland remained at 38% with an almost equal number (36%) not knowing.

Sinn Fein also needs to win over opinion in the Republic of Ireland, which has fluctuated in recent years. In 2015, a poll commissioned by RTÉ and the BBC asked the Irish population what their choice for the constitutional status of Northern Ireland would be in the short and medium terms. While reunification was the preferred option, it only gathered 36% of favourable opinions, with 35% opting for a devolved Assembly and Executive and 9% opting for Northern Ireland to remain part of the UK. Interestingly, the ratio of those who did not know was quite high, at 17%. But when the question moved to that of a United Ireland within the lifetime of the respondents, the proportion rose to 66%, with an even higher per-centage of people not sure (20% don't know). Finally, on whether respondents were prepared to pay higher taxes to see reunification happen, 31% answered positively, while 44% were against and 20% did not know. The following year, another poll asked a more direct question: 'is it time for a United Ireland?' to which 46% said Yes, 32% No and 20% didn't know. Support was the highest among the 25–34 age group.[26] In May 2019, after the local and EU elections, an RTÉ exit poll found that this time 65% of respondents were in favour of a United Ireland, whereas 15% were against it.

Overall, then, public opinion has been shifting and fluctuating. The last time the Irish electorate had their say on the future of Northern Ireland was in 1998, when they were called upon to approve the constitutional change that the implementation of the GFA generated: the amendment of articles 2 and 3 of the constitution, which laid a claim, albeit aspirational, from the Irish Republic over the whole of the island and its constituent parts. The debate was not particularly heated. It seemed that the Irish public was largely appreciative of the efforts of both governments and of the parties to reach an agreement. The results showed resounding support (94%) for the amendment of both clauses.

Sinn Féin is aware that it cannot, on its own, bring about the necessary changes that will lead to a referendum on a United Ireland. It needs to build strong support, both within the populations of North and South and within other political parties. The idea of a 'pan-Nationalist alliance' that was key to the peace process[27] is a format that Sinn Féin is willing to consider.[28] Indeed, the party is convinced that the likelihood of a British Prime Minister calling a referendum in the North is small, although not impossible as they agreed to one such referendum in Scotland in 2014 (Farrell, interview, 2020). However, building a strong alliance that would include all those in favour of Irish unity would strengthen their hand.

> For the first time Nationalist and Republican MPs out-number Unionist MPs. Our parties are pro-Irish unity and they have been gaining in the last number of elections in the north. But absolutely, we also do need an Irish government that is in favour of having a unity referendum. But at the end, it does come down to the Secretary of State, and really, in my view, that comes down to the British Prime Minister to decide. (Farrell, interview, 2020)

The legacy of the Troubles

The past is the past, there is no future to be found there.
(Mary Lou McDonald, *IT*, 26/02/20)

Reporting on Sinn Féin's electoral performance in the
2020 general election in the Republic of Ireland, most
of the foreign media continued to describe the party as
the former political wing of the IRA. This is an expedient shortcut that not only does not reflect a political
reality, but might never really have done so. However,
for decades, Sinn Féin was seen as the more visible and
presentable side of the IRA. While there is no doubt that
in many instances there was a duality of membership
and a convergence in discourse and objectives, Sinn Féin
was not a mere political front for the IRA. It had its own
strategies, agendas and personnel. It wholeheartedly supported the actions of its counterpart, but it also contributed to the political debate within the movement and at
large. Ultimately, it was Sinn Féin's vision that prevailed.
Arguably, without its support, the IRA would probably

not have sustained its military operations for so long. But nor would it have agreed to a ceasefire and to decommissioning. Dismissing or simplifying the party as a mere sidekick to a paramilitary organisation ignores the fact that no matter how close the ties it maintained with the IRA, Sinn Féin was, throughout the Troubles, a fully operational political party.

Constructing a post-IRA narrative

Undeniably, the relationship between Sinn Féin and the IRA is still unclear for many politicians and observers alike. In 2015, two former members of the IRA were killed in Belfast. Both these deaths were part of a cycle of murders linked to former paramilitaries. But what made these incidents stand out, according to the Police Service of Northern Ireland (PSNI) Chief Constable, was that this time, the perpetrators were members of the Provisional IRA. This assessment shook the Irish political world. The Provisional IRA was supposed to have disbanded, with the final act of decommissioning in 2005 and the assessment of the International Monitoring Commission on paramilitaries, which had categorically stated in 2011 that it had gone 'out of business' and therefore that the Army Council, the ruling body of the IRA, had also ceased to exist (IMC, 2011, 15).

As a result, the British government commissioned the PSNI, in conjunction with MI5, to investigate and assess the 'structures, roles and purpose of paramilitary groups in Northern Ireland'. The subsequent report, published on 19 October 2015, unambiguously stated that while the IRA was indeed committed to the peace process, the Army Council was still in existence and continued to supervise political decisions made by Sinn Féin (PSNI/MI5, HMSO, 2015). This accusation has since repeatedly been levelled at the party. In February 2020, shortly after the general election, the Garda Commissioner confirmed the PSNI's assessment that the Army Council still held a strong influence over the party. Some political leaders, such as Taoiseach Leo Varadkar, urged the President of Sinn Féin, Mary Lou McDonald, to 'disband the Army Council' (*II*, 21/02/20), an injunction to which she had already partially replied by stating that 'no one was pulling [her] strings' (*The Journal*, 06/02/20). However, no matter how many times or in what terms Sinn Féin leaders deny this, the suspicion runs high, particularly among Unionist politicians. Steve Aiken, leader of the Ulster Unionist Party, therefore considers that 'Anybody who has any knowledge at all of what's happening in Northern Ireland politics and also in the Republic would be quite clear that the Army Council is still dictating the process [...] None of us considers that Sinn Féin is a truly independent political party as the rest of us would understand it' (Aiken, interview, April 2020).

Sinn Féin is adamant that these allegations are part of an overall agenda to undermine the party's political advances and to question its credibility as a political force. But whichever way Sinn Féin spins these accusations, the legacy of the IRA remains one of the challenges with which it has had to contend on its road to political success. The party does not deny its past support for the paramilitary group, and still maintains that its presence was a necessity within a specific context. The IRA's actions and its leaders' involvement with the most controversial chapters of the last fifty years remain a shadow that Sinn Féin has not yet succeeded in dispelling.

After the IRA left the scene, in the summer of 2005, with the final act of decommissioning and its assessment that the war was over, Republicans had to find a way to talk about their former ally in a manner that would be both acceptable to their constituents and not offensive to their opponents. Indeed, it was important to come up with a narrative that would portray the former paramilitaries in a positive light while not antagonising further those who had directly and indirectly suffered at their hands or as a result of their operations. This was a fraught exercise, bound to have limitations as far as their opponents were concerned. The fault line is still profound, not only in Northern Ireland, where most of the paramilitaries' actions took place, but also in the Republic where resentment against them still runs deep.

The post-IRA narrative was largely predicated upon a time factor. There was a sell-by date to the armed strategy, beyond which all new emanations of violent organisations were deemed illegitimate. The end of the violent era was marked by the IRA's acceptance of the GFA and the ending of its own operations, which cleared the way for what were deemed democratic conditions within which it was possible to fully operate politically. As Gerry Adams stated when reacting to the assassination of a PSNI officer in 2010 by dissident republicans: 'The war is over. The IRA is gone. The IRA embraced, facilitated and supported the Peace Process' (*AP*, 14/04/11). Hence, all dissident organisations are seen as misguided and illegitimate. Sinn Féin spokespersons do not miss an opportunity to condemn operations that would have once been greeted with respect or at least condoned as part of an inevitable strategy. They remind their new opponents that the conditions for armed struggle are strictly defined by, and confined to, a set of circumstances which no longer prevail. Republicans hailed the GFA as creating such favourable circumstances, notwithstanding the many obstacles that would need to be overcome, and their contribution to the peace process, provided the prerequisite context for a full and unconditional embracing of political strategies.

The dominant narrative that Sinn Féin pushed over the last thirty years places the IRA, and Republicans in general, at the heart of the peace process. This was restated in 2019 by Mary Lou McDonald when celebrating the 25th anniversary of the IRA ceasefire, which in her view, together with the 'peace process that followed, asserted the primacy of politics and the rights of citizens. The actions of the IRA demonstrated that political differences are not intractable and conflict need not be inevitable' (PR, 30/08/19). However, such statements are ambivalent, as by placing the IRA at the centre of the peace process and identifying it as its main facilitator, they undermine the paramilitary organisation's responsibility in the conflict.

The discursive strategy deployed to justify the existence of the IRA and simultaneously legitimise the end of the armed strategy was founded on a syllogism: the IRA fought to bring about a situation where it would be possible to fight by democratic means, thus the IRA are considered the champions of democracy. While this could be seen as a contradiction in terms, the IRA being by definition an undemocratic organisation (its secrecy, the election of its leaders, the recruitment of members taking place in total opacity for obvious security reasons among others), it was nonetheless the argument frequently developed in the years following the final act of decommissioning and the subsequent declaration that the 'war was over' (*AP*, 28/07/05). Hence, in Adams' view, 'when a democratic and peaceful alternative to armed struggle was created, the IRA left the stage' (*AP*, 30/07/10). Nevertheless, by engaging in electoral politics with the 'Armalite and ballot box' strategy, Sinn Féin had acknowledged in the early 1980s that democratic means such as electoral processes were also effective, thus making the above argument convoluted. However, following the Republican reasoning, there were three stages to the strategy. The first, in the 1970s, had political violence at its core. The second, from the 1980s, saw the introduction of a hybrid approach, with a mix of both military and political strategies. Both enabled the third and final stage, which was entirely fought on the political front with the backing of the IRA until it finally left the scene.

The narrative was further elaborated to shed a light on the IRA that both connected it to a long line of republican organisations and reaffirmed its unique contribution to the lives of those it purported to protect. The main lenses through which the IRA was presented were as defenders, people's army and soldiers. These themes were developed on a regular basis throughout the conflict, most notably in the early years with the construction of a powerful propaganda machine and a distinct discourse.

The IRA were, first and foremost, seen as defenders. They stood against the injustice of the Unionist, or in Republican parlance, Stormont regime and, most of all, against British power in all its representations (military, political or cultural). They defended Catholics against the 'pogroms' carried out in the summer of 1970 (*AP*, 2/7/10). They sacrificed themselves and 'made a brighter future possible' according to McGuinness (*AP*, 30/7/10). The irony of portraying in such positive terms an organisation responsible for almost half of the deaths throughout the conflict was probably lost on those who were convinced that armed action was liberating. Republicans believed that the IRA was a people's army, people being defined as 'those anonymous individuals who helped the struggle, and who fed and looked after or sheltered Volunteers' (*AP*, 2/7/10).

The depiction of the IRA as an altruistic organisation whose members were prepared to sacrifice their lives for a cause contributed to playing down its responsibility in the conflict. They were presented as a revolutionary force, but by no means 'warmongers'. They produced their own heroes, the pinnacle of whom are of course the hunger strikers. As Sinn Féin TD Caoimhghín Ó Caoláin stated, 'For my generation of republicans, 1981 was our Easter Week, our 1916' (*AP*, 6/08/13). The secrecy of the organisation further shrouded the IRA members in mystery, affording them a quasi-mystic dimension. They were presented as both selfless (the names of their members and leaders will never be disclosed and thus they did not get involved for personal motives, gains or glory) and all-powerful. Veteran republican Jim Gibney once explained in an interview with the American magazine *Frontline* that: 'The real praise must go to an unknown group of people who will never step up to the podium to receive the accolade they are most definitely entitled to – a group of people who were prepared to listen to Gerry Adams and Martin McGuinness and then take their own counsel' (*AP*, 30/08/14).

Finally, the IRA were undefeated. Adams declared in 2015: 'the reality is that the IRA was never defeated and that again and again it was Irish republicans, including the IRA leadership, which took bold steps to bolster the Peace Process and to maintain positive political momentum' (*AP*, 15/07/15). This trope, developed as soon as the first ceasefire was announced, was designed to enable the IRA to keep face, or rather, to confirm the superiority of its struggle, both militarily and morally, while assuring supporters that they had reached a win-win situation. While the GFA might have seemed, at best, unsatisfactory to those who criticised Sinn Féin for its U-turn on the so-called internal solution and the copper-fastening of partition, Sinn Féin was able to spin this discourse to present it as a victory attributable to the IRA.

Commemorations and funerals

The elaboration of this narrative was a perilous rhetorical exercise. Indeed, it was important not to antagonise those who had supported the IRA, who had dedicated their lives to the organisation, counted victims among their circles, spent time in prison, or simply had believed that the goalpost was reunification, nothing less. This constituency, while certainly declining, is still a force to be reckoned with. The Troubles and the experiences of those who lived through those three decades are still regularly commemorated by Republicans, in many different manners. A 2016 study showed that between 2009 and 2014, the majority of commemorative events (1,036, i.e. 59.6%) were organised by Republicans, of which more than half (676) by 'mainstream' republicans'. The authors also noted that 'although parades formed a part of 401 republican commemorations, proving the single most popular form of commemoration, the majority of public memory work used other methods. Many of these were relatively low key such as discussions, lectures and talks' (Brown & Grant, 2016, 146).

Commemorations are an integral part of Sinn Féin's activities. West Dublin Sinn Féin TD Aengus Ó Snodaigh explains that they are important insofar as they maintain the link between past and present, but they are not about 'replicating the past, we are not tied to the past' (Ó Snodaigh, interview, August 2020). Hardly a month goes by without a leading Sinn Féin figure attending such events, which provide a platform from which the party can deliver its message and further anchor its vision of the past and the future. History is an ever-present dimension within Sinn Féin's discourse and strategies. The manner in which the past is interpreted is highly political, as it determines the way in which the party situates its struggle and justifies its past and current choices. The narratives that are elaborated are predicated upon a 'remembered past', as opposed to the 'actual past', as this allows 'selective 'remembering' and 'forgetting' processes that feed into collective memory, political identity and group boundaries' (Hearty, 2017, 55). Thus, the people or events that are remembered indicate the route that Republicans have travelled and the objectives that they mean to pursue. Some of these relate to their recent past, others go back in time and reveal a vision of history that legitimises their actions and their choices, and that place Republicans on the right side of history, as opposed to those who have stood in their way. The controversy surrounding the commemoration of the Royal Irish Constabulary (RIC) in 2020 was a good example, not only of how divisive history still is, but of the manner in which it is still open to radically different interpretations that suit specific needs. The RIC and the Dublin Metropolitan Police (DMP) were the forces that served in Ireland prior to independence, and that, for many, were associated with the British Empire and seen as a colonial force, on the side of the oppressor. The planned commemoration for some 500 members who died between the Easter Rising and the War of Independence was part of the events of the Decade of Centenaries.[1] This was particularly controversial as the RIC are still viewed in some quarters as having symbolised the British repression which followed the Rising and the setting up of the first Dáil (National Assembly) in 1919, particularly in view of the fact that the reserve forces which were integrated into the RIC, the Black and Tans and the Auxiliaries, were responsible for some of the worst massacres of the period. The Expert Advisory Group, in charge of the organisation of the various events, had not recommended an official commemoration, rather 'specific initiatives to commemorate the RIC and the DMP and to acknowledge their place in history' (*The Journal*, 07/01/20). The planned event, in Dublin Castle, was eventually cancelled given the controversy that ensued, with Sinn Féin stating that 'in no other State would those who facilitated the suppression of national freedom be commemorated by the State' (PR, 06/01/20), and Fianna Fáil, while less scathing, proposed the holding of an academic conference rather than a standalone commemoration. But the episode showed how entrenched positions still are. Minister for Justice Charlie O'Flanagan summarised his government's position when he explained that 'The horrific record of the Black and Tans and Auxiliaries is well known. But there were thousands of other officers who behaved with dignity and honour in serving their communities. And we should not seek to airbrush these people from our history' (BBC, 08/01/20). However, the controversy, according to Varadkar, had pushed back the prospect of a United Ireland as it showed the difficulty in recognising the heritage of 'one million people on the island who identify as British and as being from a unionist background' (*IT*, 08/01/20).

Republican commemorations are targeted and concern those whose narratives are firmly rooted within their vision of history. However, Aengus Ó Snodaigh insists that these events need not be celebratory, and that most focus on individuals as opposed to specific episodes or operations (Ó Snodaigh, interview, August 2020). It is important that the movement is seen to be all encompassing in its remembrance choices. In October 2019, Gerry Adams spoke at the 100th anniversary of the birth of Sinn Féin's Vice-President from 1970 to 1976, Máire Drumm, who was killed while in hospital by a Loyalist organisation. Adams took this opportunity to remind the attendance not only of her heroic and patriotic stances, but of her unconditional support for the armed campaign, ending his speech with a direct quote from Drumm: 'Long live the IRA! God save Ireland!' (PR, 13/10/19). In an equally grandiose style, MEP Martina Anderson paid tribute to the hunger strikers and warned the UK that 'you can lie all you want, but we know the truth, and the truth is that your days in Ireland are numbered' (PR, 04/08/19).

Commemorations therefore represent a platform from which party leaders put across a specific message relevant at a specific time. In the wake of the assassination of journalist Lyra McKee in Derry in April 2019, Deputy First Minister Michelle O'Neill used her address to the 1916 Rising commemoration to call on dissident republicans to disband. That same year, Mary Lou McDonald warned her audience that the 'political stalemate [could not]

continue' (PR, 21/04/19), in a reference to the 2017 suspension of the Northern Ireland institutions. It is also
the occasion for the speakers to look at their history,
sometimes taking liberties with the narrative. McDonald
thus explained, in her address at the centenary of the
Soloheadbeg ambush in Tipperary[2] that the 'majority of
the people of this island had spoken at the ballot box.
They voted for Sinn Féin and they voted for equality, for
liberty and to break the link with Britain' (PR, 19/01/19).
While Sinn Féin won an overwhelming majority of the
seats in 1918 (73 out of 105), it obtained 46.9% of the
vote, a considerable percentage indeed contrasted with
the performance of their Nationalist rival of the time,
the Irish Parliamentary party, but not an overall majority. The modern spin that McDonald put on the meaning
of the vote ('equality') also serves to anchor Sinn Féin's
current priorities in a historical context. Pearse Doherty
used a similar type of rhetorical tool when he connected
the fiftieth anniversary of the Northern Ireland Civil
Rights movement to current issues: 'An Irish Language
Act, marriage equality, women's reproductive health, and
legacy rights, are the 2018 version of "one person, one
vote"' (PR, 11/11/18), attempting to put a modern spin on
a slogan better known as 'one man one vote', but possibly
too gendered for a contemporary audience.

Commemorations serve a very specific purpose: they
are designed to cultivate a counter-memory to the British
account of events and to institute a dominant narrative
within Republican circles (Hopkins, 2015). They play a
dual role, being, in a post-conflict situation, 'just as likely

to be a way of perpetuating and recalibrating divisions, as [they are] likely to lead to reconciliation' (O'Callaghan, 2016). Some of the individuals commemorated, however, raise more questions than others. In October 2018, a service for Thomas Begley, who died in the premature explosion of his own device on the Shankill Road on 23 October 1993, which killed 10 people and injured 57, was attended by 200 people, among whom were a number of senior local republicans and Sinn Féin representatives. Such events are intrinsically controversial, no matter how sensitive the approach. McDonald's assessment that 'for us to respect each other and for us to begin the process of healing and reconciliation, we have to allow for remembrance by everybody, by all sides' (IT, 26/10/18) might not have been entirely convincing for those who were directly affected by the bombing. These occasions can be seen as an attempt from the organisation to atone for the event. On the twentieth anniversary of the Shankill bombing, Declan Kearney had, at least partly, taken responsibility on behalf of his organisation: 'Victims were created on and by all sides: by republicans, by the British State and its forces and agencies, and by unionists. All sides were part of the context in which the conflict occurred and continued. Sadly, that past cannot be changed or undone. Neither can it be disowned by republicans or anyone else' (AP, 12/10/13). But such occasions can also be interpreted as glorifying armed struggle. The main speaker in the 2018 tribute to Begley was involved in the operation and described his dead companion as an 'eager, determined, committed and cool volunteer', while local councillor Seanad Walsh talked of 'a peaceful political way forward [...] which had been opened up by those who gave their lives for Irish freedom' (*IT*, 27/10/18).

Memory is an essential tool in the construction of a national narrative, one which enables the party to be in control of what is remembered and what is forgotten. Commemorations are a duty, an adaptation of the concept of the duty of memory (*devoir de mémoire*) which surfaced in public debate in the late 1980s and which places victims at the centre of a moral duty by individuals, groups or states to remember. In Sinn Féin's narrative, however, the victims of those who are commemorated are not necessarily prioritised, which means that the past can be interpreted in such a way as to avoid, or at least undermine, the responsibility of the perpetrators of violence. Just like Sinn Féin opposes any notion of a hierarchy of victims, it is equally opposed to a hierarchy of perpetrators, as it sees all those who acted in the name of the IRA as being worthy of remembrance.

Funerals play a similar function to that of commemoration, and until the early 1990s, they were an opportunity for the Republican movement to defy the authorities and on occasion to stage a show of military strength. This often led to clashes between the security forces and Republican sympathisers, although the Republican movement decided in 1987 to tone down the more controversial aspects somewhat, such as the firing of a volley of shots over coffins. With the peace process, the nature of funerals has dramatically changed and there is no longer a paramilitary presence as such. But as Scull notes, 'funerals have always proved crucial to sustaining the republican tradition' (2020). Such an opportunity was created by the funeral of veteran Bobby Storey, in June 2020, although the event would come back to haunt Republicans for the months to come. Storey was famous for his contribution to the so-called 'great escape', when thirty-eight men fled from the Maze prison in 1983. More importantly, he was seen as a loyal supporter of the leadership who took the movement through the peace process. According to the *Irish Times*, 'They provided the strategy, he provided the muscle to ensure they got their way' (*IT*, 30/06/20). The funeral seemed carefully choreographed, with streets lined with men (and a handful of women) soberly dressed in white shirts, black ties and black trousers, walking in rhythm to the sound of a horn pipe. The fact that the funeral of a prominent figure such as Storey, linked to the IRA and to a now seemingly remote past, attracted such a high number of people (estimated at 'hundreds' by the *Irish News* and 'up to 1,800 by the *Irish Independent*) clearly shows how relevant and important the IRA remains within Republican circles. Party President Mary Lou McDonald praised Storey for his contribution to the peace process, showing how impossible it would still be for any leader to deviate from the orthodoxy of the party on the peace process narrative. Gerry Adams had a slightly convoluted message for those who had come to pay a tribute to Storey, reminding them that 'Sinn Féin is controlled by no one. We're a democratic, open organisation', while simultaneously being 'glad and proud that Bobby and other former Volunteers are part of what we are' (PR, 30/05/20).

The funeral provoked a controversy centred on the breach of the COVID-19 restrictions in place in Northern Ireland, which at the time only permitted a maximum of thirty people at outdoor gatherings. The fact that so many people attended, according to Galway TD Mairéad Farrell, was not the party's doing, as 'we tried streaming online and get people to watch it online rather than to come out in the streets. But Bobby was an extremely important person for us'. However, when asked about the spontaneity of a procession where hundreds of people walked in line, all dressed in a similar manner, she explained: 'if you're aware of what it's like in West Belfast, that would be a common thing. That's just the political reality of West Belfast. People would wear black and white at funerals' (Farrell, interview, September 2020). While the explanation might not be entirely convincing, there is obviously a delicate balance to strike in such circumstances. There is little doubt that Sinn Féin leaders were aware that they would be challenged over their presence at such an event. A month earlier, in June 2020, Sinn Féin TD Pa Daly had attended a funeral 'out of the respect that I had for Seán Máirtín and his family' (*IE*, 4/6/20). His decision was in breach of the COVID-19 restrictions, which only allowed travel within a 5 km perimeter and thus generated a small controversy. These incidents feed into an already well-trodden narrative according to which Sinn Féin, by placing itself above the law, demonstrates its questionable democratic credentials. DUP MP Gregory Campbell saw the Storey funeral as a clear sign of Sinn Féin's close ties to its past and to the IRA, which in his view 'indicated to most of us that we have a considerable way to go yet' (Campbell, interview, August 2020). Fianna Fáil leader and Taoiseach Micheál Martin, while initially avoiding getting drawn into a controversy, assessed the situation in stark terms in October 2020. According to him, 'People were summoned from the length and breadth of the country to attend to make a statement [...] around the war as they'd call it', thereby 'defying' public health guidelines (*IT*, 24/10/20).

However, leaders such as Mary Lou McDonald and Michelle O'Neill might have been caught between a rock and a hard place. Not attending Storey's funeral would have reflected poorly on their qualities as leaders of a movement still steeped in that past. Attending meant exposing themselves to the criticisms that followed and that were accompanied by calls for the Northern Ireland Deputy First Minister's resignation. Michelle O'Neill's apologies to the families that were denied the opportunity to grieve their dead throughout the lockdown restrictions could be construed as an admission of the ill-advised choice she made to attend the funeral, although she claimed in her message that being present at a requiem mass was permitted, as was following a funeral cortege of up to thirty people. The incident momentarily isolated Sinn Féin from its Assembly colleagues as all four other parties (UUP, DUP, Alliance and SDLP) called for explanations. Those provided by Pat Sheehan in Stormont, when responding to a motion tabled by the DUP, related to the fact that Republican funerals had 'been the subject of attacks on many occasions', thus largely avoiding the main question (Sheehan, YouTube, 07/07/20). The controversy was exploited by DUP Minister Edwin Poots in order to oppose the proposed lockdown measures to fight against the COVID-19 pandemic in October 2020. The claim that 'a lot of the problems started after the Bobby Storey funeral ... and people in that community saw the breaking of the rules' (*Irish News*, 17/10/20) was swiftly condemned by all other parties who pointed to the Minister for Agriculture's attempts to 'sectarianise' the COVID-19 pandemic. Months later, a police investigation which had been in the making since June 2020 and which involved twenty-four Sinn Féin representatives concluded that no one would be prosecuted, prompting First Minister Arlene Foster to call for the resignation of the Chief Constable. The controversy was also one of the factors that ignited the riots which shook Northern Ireland over the 2021 Easter period, with some within Loyalism expressing doubts as to the impartiality of the PSNI and feeling vindicated in their long-held conviction that the peace process was biased in favour of Nationalists.

Political damage

When Gerry Adams stood down as President of Sinn Féin in 2018 to be replaced by Mary Lou McDonald, a new era was undeniably set in motion. The references to the IRA, less and less frequent since the middle of the decade,

became from then on largely absent from Sinn Féin's discourse. As the new President declared to her party congress (Ard Fheis) in 2018: 'The truth is, my friends, I
won't fill Gerry's shoes [...] But the news is that I brought
my own' (*Irish News*, 16/5/20).

This was certainly good news for those within the
party who were in charge of extinguishing the many
fires that were lit by revelations which put the leaders
of the movement in awkward situations. Adams was at
the heart of most of the controversies that shook the
party throughout the 2010s. He certainly catalysed the
admiration of his own supporters and the hatred of both
those who felt personally betrayed by his change of direction and those who held him directly responsible for the
violence committed throughout the conflict. He also possibly mismanaged his narrative about his own past, as his
repeated denials over his involvement in the IRA never
convinced his many detractors for a number of reasons.
His leadership of a party with such symbiotic ties with
the paramilitary organisation, his closeness to individuals known for their IRA past, and his ability to have a
direct line with the Army Council and to influence major
decisions certainly pointed to a connection. While his
past would still have been questioned, his admission to
having played a role within the IRA might have gained
him a level of trust. Martin McGuinness played his cards
differently. He availed of the opportunity afforded by the
Saville Enquiry[3] to admit that at the time of the events,
he was second-in-command of the Derry Battalion (*IT*,
02/05/01). This 'coming out' probably helped to clear the

air and dispel some ambiguity. McGuinness's funeral in March 2017 was attended by thousands, including current and past leaders, national and international figures (among whom Enda Kenny, Taoiseach at the time, President Michael D. Higgins and former US President Bill Clinton), showing the respect that he had managed to command, in spite of his connection with the IRA. Adams' past, on the other hand, raised many questions for his political colleagues. 'There isn't a guard in the country who doesn't believe that you weren't in the IRA', said Fianna Fáil leader Micheál Martin in a TV debate, to which Adams suggested that he bring the evidence he had to the Guards (*II*, 15/02/16). Labour Tánaiste Joan Bruton reinforced this point, stressing that he relied on a 'distinguished set of friends' that would 'terrify the life out of most decent people' (*IT*, 17/02/16). Adams' role as Chief of Staff is treated as an open secret. Interestingly, however, these allegations never deterred the Sinn Féin President's electorate, as he topped the poll in his Louth constituency both in the 2011 and 2016 general elections. Perhaps, as noted by senior political commentator Vincent Browne, this is not how Adams will ultimately be remembered by his supporters:

> We all know Gerry Adams was one of the leading figures in the IRA for a long time and it is no surprise he denies that, for to do otherwise would leave him open to criminal prosecution and, probably, civil suits. We also all know of the complicity of Gerry Adams in legions of IRA atrocities, atrocities that probably would have happened anyway, with or without him. But it was Gerry Adams

who, more than any other single person, was responsible for delivering the most significant political achievement of Irish history for generations: the peace agreement on Northern Ireland. In terms of achievement, no other figure in Irish public life rates even close to him. (*IT*, 24/02/16).

Despite firmly embracing the peace process, dissociating the party from its image as a supporter of armed violence proved a challenging task on both sides of the border. Nevertheless, gradually, the very name of the paramilitary organisation was expunged from official Sinn Féin documents, as the last time the IRA was mentioned in the electoral manifestos was in 2007 (both for the Assembly and the Dáil elections), where the final decommissioning act of 2005 was described as 'a historic unilateral initiative that has opened unprecedented democratic opportunities' (Sinn Féin, Dáil Manifesto, 2007, 19). The change in leadership undoubtedly contributed to shedding some of the cobwebs from the past. Aengus Ó Snodaigh admits that the presence of McGuinness or Adams at the head of the party 'allowed opponents to categorise us as militant' while the new generation at the head of the party means that 'there is no longer a charge against us about the association with militarism'. However, he does point to the fact that for some, Adams was the reason people voted for the party, as he was seen as 'the one to lead the party from militarism to peace' (Ó Snodaigh, interview, August 2020).

But the past keeps intruding with the present in many different ways. Sinn Féin has developed a well-oiled strategy for defending or justifying past IRA actions, in order to maintain the narrative of the IRA as the people's army. This was no easy task when having to explain or atone for past actions that could not in any way be justified as being part of the 'struggle'. One of the main lines of argument is to make a clear distinction between the party and the paramilitary organisation. This is a perilous exercise as it is imperative not to shift the blame of specific actions onto the IRA in order to sustain the overall positive image nurtured by Sinn Féin. Throughout the decommissioning controversy, whenever Sinn Féin was challenged over the slow pace of the process, Republican spokespersons repeated on many occasions that as a party, it had no weapons and thus could not be held directly accountable for the IRA's failure to hand in their arsenal (Maillot, 2005). Dealing with controversial aspects of IRA actions requires the ability to strike a balance between denouncing such acts while not condemning the organisation as a whole. This was the case, for instance, with paramilitary-style attacks which were carried out by organisations from all sides throughout the conflict, and that continue to be perpetrated by some groups, albeit on a smaller scale, targeting individuals who are punished for so-called 'anti-social behaviour'. During the conflict, these attacks were justified by the IRA as a necessity in areas where the law and order representatives had little, if any, legitimacy. The republican narrative was that the IRA had taken on this role under pressure from the community to fill the vacuum in policing and had done so reluctantly, as this role was, in Adams' view, 'a major distraction from the organisation's central function' (*AP*, 19/10/14). However, the problematic aspects of this role, not least the fact that individuals were taking the law into their own hands and handing down sentences that resulted in physical harm, permanent wounding, exiling and some-times executing, were somehow brushed aside during the peace process to focus on more pressing matters such as the decommissioning of paramilitary weapons and prisoner release. However, according to a medical study, these attacks 'still represent a significant burden on the health service resources, together with the associated morbidity which impacts on the public purse in the form of disability living allowance and compensation claims. The psychological impact on both victims and witnesses of these crimes remains indeterminable' (Napier et al., 2017). Indeed, according to the support group 'Ending the Harm', 389 such attacks occurred between the years 2015 and 2020, with 11 shootings and 39 assaults for 2020 alone (www.endingtheharm.com).

However, if paramilitary-style attacks were in some instances explained as a necessity when law and order had failed communities, there was no possible way to see rape or sexual abuse in a similar light, even in the most convoluted manner. In recent years, among the most damaging revelations for Republicans were those con-cerning some members of the IRA who had used their positions and power to sexually abuse men and women within their own community. Several victims came forward in the early 2010s, one of whom, Maria Cahill, was the great niece of former IRA leader Joe Cahill. Still more damaging was the fact that she openly accused Sinn Féin, in a BBC documentary, of a cover-up operation (BBC, *Spotlight*, 2014). Sexual abuses were perpetrated by all sides throughout the conflict, albeit not on a systemic or large scale. Most documented cases are those abuses committed by the British Army and within the prisons, notably the case of the Armagh strip searches[4] (O'Keefe, 2006). But this issue was seldom publicly discussed. Researchers contend that 'conflict-related sexual violence (CRSV) are issues that remain marginal to the Northern Ireland transition from conflict' (O'Rourke & Swaine, 2017, 1302). As in the case of the military-style attacks or the Disappeared (see following section), the victims were all from within the community. To make things worse for Sinn Féin, when these allegations surfaced, the IRA was no longer there to take the blame, putting party spokespersons directly in the firing line. Some leaders were alleged to have covered up the abuses and allowed the perpetrators to go unpunished, at best forcing them into exile. Such allegations were swiftly denied, but the inadequacy of the explanation provided, for instance, by Martin McGuinness in 2014, according to whom 'the IRA were totally ill-equipped to deal with allegations of anti-social behaviour, criminality or sexual abuse' and repeated, verbatim, by Adams in the Dáil ('the IRA was ill-equipped to deal with such matters', PR, 22/10/14) demonstrated how damaging these contentions were for the party, whose blind spot when it came to properly assessing the IRA's role in its relationship to civil society was made all the more obvious. The subtext was that the IRA could have dealt with these allegations better, which was problematic on a number of levels. Indeed, it showed the failure of Republicans to question the IRA's legitimacy in that particular role. Equally problematic was the fact that it addressed the issue from the perspective of the perpetrator, not the victims.

Mary Lou McDonald opted for a similar strategy, but in a more articulate language, expressing an 'unreserved apology and deep regret that procedures of the mandatory reporting of abuse allegations were not in place at the time' (*IT*, 20/11/18). However, it was unclear what procedures she was referring to. These statements were nevertheless a good indication of the need for the Sinn Féin leaders to tread a thin line between defending reprehensible actions that discredit the organisation, and not demystifying the IRA which remains so closely associated to the history and credentials of the party. This might have been the reason why Adams, when apologising to the victims of sexual abuse, chose to focus not so much on the acts themselves, but on the manner in which these accusations were dealt with: 'I have acknowledged the failure of the IRA to deal properly with these difficult issues and, for that, I have apologised'. Interestingly, however, what remained at the centre of the debate, the fact that IRA members were accused of perpetrating those abuses, was not fully acknowledged by senior Republican leaders. At best, Adams admitted that 'Some [legacy cases of abuse] also may have involved IRA Volunteers' (*AP*, 19/10/14).

Apologies

Apologies are an important tool, as they have the potential to trigger forgiveness, and they suggest admission of guilt (Lundy & Roston, 2016). Public apologies are considered an integral part of restorative justice. In the early stages of the peace process, the first paramilitaries to publicly apologise were the loyalist organisations who, when announcing the ceasefire on behalf of the Combined Loyalist Military Command in October 1994, expressed 'true and abject remorse' to the families of all innocent victims of the troubles (CAIN, CLMC Ceasefire statement, 1994). The British have also officially apologised twice for past wrongdoings: Tony Blair in February 1997 for the Famine, David Cameron in 2010 for Bloody Sunday.

The IRA, for its part, was slower to embark on the journey of public apologies. The first time it actually expressed remorse was through a press statement in 1999, when the process of recovering the remains of the Disappeared, those sixteen people whose bodies were concealed after being abducted and assassinated, mostly in the 1970s, was put in motion.[5] On this occasion, the IRA stated: 'We are sorry that the suffering of those families has continued for so long. We wish to apologise for the grief caused. Our intention in initiating our investigation has been to rectify this injustice, for which we accept full responsibility' (AP, 01/04/99). The apology was problematic, however, for a number of reasons. First, it centred on the time it had taken the organisation to admit to these disappearances, but not on the killings themselves or on the disappearance of the bodies. Secondly, these disappearances would, for the years to come, still be presented as 'acts of war' (Dempster, 2016). Finally, not all remains were found, and the sincerity of the IRA's engagement with the process was questioned on a number of occasions. Nevertheless, this was the first time that the organisation had attempted to repair some of its past actions.

The only formal IRA apology was issued in 2002 and was addressed to all non-combatants on the anniversary of Bloody Friday, when on 21 July 1972, 9 people were killed and 130 injured after the IRA detonated more than 20 bombs within a few minutes of each other in Belfast City Centre. The questions that arise, however, are concerned with the value of such apologies, with the purpose that they serve in political terms, and with their capacity to mitigate the hurt and suffering that victims of those tragedies experienced, as well as advancing the agenda of reconciliation. Public apologies by prominent politicians are highly mediated and thus become a newsworthy story. Apologising as a discursive strategy can offer an insight into what is perceived as acceptable or not within the dominant political discourse, but also within the political circles where those statements are made. However, while apologies from Republicans have generally been quite scarce, they do perform an important role, in that they are, at least, an admission of guilt (Cairns et al., 2004).

The fundamental question, therefore, is the value that those whom the apologies target ascribe to them.

MacLachlan notes that 'the limits of public apology as a vehicle for demonstrating the apologizer's trustworthiness go a long way to explaining half of the paradox of apologies, namely, widespread public dissatisfaction and even condemnation (MacLachlan, 2015, 447). The 2002 IRA apology is a good case in point. A 2007 study looked at newspaper coverage of the organisation's statement in order to measure its reception and impact. The findings indicated that it was recurrently deemed 'inadequate' or 'too little too late', as well as politically expedient and self-serving. This was mitigated by a more positive interpretation, seeing the IRA statement as a welcome sign that the organisation was accepting blame and showing remorse, thus signalling a move forward. The study also highlighted the gap in perception of Nationalist and Unionist readerships, with the former tending to embrace the more positive themes (e.g. 'moving forward', 'responsibility') and the latter inclined to endorse the more negative themes (e.g. 'too little too late', 'political expediency'). While this might seem self-evident and predictable, it does point to one fundamental dimension: apologies on the part of Republicans are only perceived as honest and acceptable within their own communities and by their own supporters (Ferguson et al., 2007).

Another form of apology that Sinn Féin has been forced to adopt is that which follows a blunder on social media or in a speech. In the wake of the 2020 general election, some comments, which were, one way or another, connected to the IRA, made by public representatives had to be mitigated by either the speaker or the party itself. In one instance, Waterford TD David Cullinane had to retract the comment he made on election night: 'What we say is, up the Republic, up the Ra, and tiocfaidh ár lá'.[6] The phrase was frequently used by the IRA and their supporters throughout the conflict and has all the characteristics of a rallying cry, but also has menacing overtones for the Unionist community, who see it as representing a triumphalist outlook for the future. And while it also has powerful connotations for Republicans, described in the Slugger O'Toole blog as 'almost religious in its intensity, promising followers a sunlit upland in an undefined future, which would make the present sacrifice all worthwhile', its appropriateness for the modern day, as observed by the writer, is questionable (06/05/20).

Mary Lou McDonald dismissed the controversy that ensued as constituting a 'distraction', much in the same way as Cullinane himself had explained that he had not sought to offend anyone, as he was talking 'about the past, they're not about the future. The IRA is gone as everybody knows, and I celebrate that, the same as anybody else' (*IT*, 10/02/20). This might have been enough for the party's supporters, but the reactions in the press show how far from being innocuous and acceptable this language can be. In a column for the *Irish Times*, former BBC journalist and author Fergal Keane wrote that the 'IRA past is not history, at least not in the sense of something that has vanished into an unmarked grave never to be heard from again' and called on McDonald to 'lead Republicanism into an honest accommodation of history' (*IT*, 17/03/20). The controversy that this generated points

to the dissonance that exists between the party's perception of recent history and that of the general environ-
ment in which it operates. Cullinane was not the first to
use this phrase in recent years. In August 2019, Martina
Anderson, who was still MEP for Northern Ireland, delivered an oration in memory of the hunger strikers, which
ended with the same expression, 'tiocfaidh ár lá'.

The Cullinane episode came in the wake of another
intense controversy which risked derailing Sinn Féin's
campaign, regarding the 2007 murder of 21-year-old Paul
Quinn. A few weeks after the event, Sinn Féin MLA
Conor Murphy who had been appointed Finance Minister
in the Northern Ireland Executive in 2020, stated that
Quinn was involved in crime, an allegation that his
parents strongly denied and for which they demanded
an apology. Quinn's murderers were never brought to
justice, although a total of twenty-three people were
arrested by both the PSNI and the Gardaí, none of whom
were charged. His parents' continued campaign ensured
that the case sporadically made the headlines, as in 2014
when the SDLP tabled a motion in Stormont to support
their efforts, and in 2017 when RTÉ dedicated one of its
Prime Time Investigation programmes to the case. When
the story resurfaced days before the general election,
Murphy eventually apologised, which helped to mitigate
the potential damage that this could have caused to the
party in the midst of an election campaign. But the episode was telling on a number of levels. It raised questions
as to why a Sinn Féin MLA felt it appropriate to comment on the supposedly criminal background of a murder

victim and then wait for thirteen years to retract such comments. Nevertheless, it did not seem to dent the support that the party was garnering in the opinion polls and which translated into a high number of first preference votes.

The relationship that the Irish electorate holds with the IRA is far from straightforward. A 2013 study carried out by historian Brian Hanley shows support for the IRA in the Republic was never solid throughout the conflict, and with the exception of specific moments such as the 1980–1981 hunger strikes, it was not seen as a legitimate organisation. But the origins of this relationship, built in great part on the myths generated after the civil war, muddied the waters. Indeed, 'the historical status attached to the IRA meant that people wanted to identify with them but felt repulsed by their actions' (Hanley, 2013, 456). The Provisional IRA was denied the legitimacy afforded to the so-called 'old IRA',[7] seen in a more favourable light. However, the comparison between the Provisionals and the old IRA, according to historian Andy Bielenberg, does not necessarily weigh in favour of the latter. His research shows for instance that the 'old IRA' were responsible for the disappearances of 62 people in Cork between 1920 and 1922, and of over 100 people nationwide, leading him to conclude that this was 'off the scale' with the Provisional IRA and that the issue of the moral superiority of the 'Old IRA' was questionable (*IT*, 20/08/18). Obviously the main difference is that the current revelations about IRA past actions concern people who are still in a position to testify or to face prosecution. Furthermore, peace and victim-centred processes are relatively recent, which means that the reality of the hurt inflicted during the War of Independence and civil war were not uncovered at the time and no avenue existed for victims to be heard or compensated.

Ultimately, however, such apologies will never be sufficient to those who still view the IRA as being entirely responsible for the conflict. As UUP leader Steve Aiken explains, 'Mary Lou McDonald would need to stand up and admit that IRA violence was wrong. David Cameron stood up and apologised for Bloody Sunday very clearly, unreservedly, but we've never had an apology from the leader of Sinn Féin to say the same thing' (Aiken, interview, April 2020). This comparison can be challenged on the basis that the terms of the comparison are unbalanced, as Cameron did not apologise for all British Army incidents. Moreover, asking Sinn Féin to apologise for all IRA violence would imply a disavowal of the IRA. It is also an unrealistic demand – and knowingly so – to make of a party whose identity has always been profoundly linked to that of the IRA.

Counter-narratives

Aiken's comment shows how much at odds Sinn Féin's narrative on the IRA is with most other discourses, on both sides of the border. Unionist politicians' antipathy for the IRA has hardly relented, as shown by the words and concepts they use to describe both members of the IRA and their campaign. For instance, Steve Aiken sees them as 'war criminals' (Aiken, interview, April 2020). The use of that expression is in itself quite telling, since Unionists would obviously strongly refute that the IRA was engaged in a war, as they were deemed an illegitimate group carrying out acts of terrorism. A few years previously, in September 2012, the DUP tabled a motion in the Assembly which called on the Irish government to apologise for its alleged role in the emergence of the IRA in a manner that would 'make reference to and acknowledge the ethnic cleansing'. The fact that it was passed by forty-seven to forty-six votes in the Assembly gave an insight into the manner in which the IRA actions were still perceived among Unionist representatives (Hansard, 17/09/12). The use of the phrase 'ethnic cleansing' is in itself a good indication of the level of anger, resentment and hurt that persists. It is also problematic, as ethnic cleansing has been used in contexts where whole sections of a population have been targeted and even eliminated. While there is still no agreed legal international definition, the closest available is that of a United Nations Commission of Experts, which sees it as 'a purposeful policy designed by one ethnic or religious group to remove by violent and terror-inspiring means the civilian population of another ethnic or religious group from certain geographic areas' (UN Office of Genocide Prevention). Whether this definition is appropriate to describe the actions of any paramilitary group in Northern Ireland is subject to question. It implies that not only was the IRA a sectarian organisation, but that it deliberately targeted Protestants to eventually dislodge them. Republicans obviously refute such a view; for them, the objective was the removal of the British presence and therefore their conflict was primarily with the British, not with the Protestants. Nevertheless, operations such as Kingsmill, where on 5 January 1976, ten Protestant workers travelling in a mini-van were killed (and one Catholic was let go) throw confusion into the debate, as the event clearly had all the hallmarks of a sectarian attack. The fact that a group called the South Armagh Republican Action Force claimed responsibility made it possible for the IRA and Republicans in general to distance themselves from such operations. However, the Historical Enquiry Team not only reaffirmed that 'The motive was purely sectarian, with each man being murdered purely because he was a Protestant' (IT, 21/06/11), but also that the group was a front for the Provisional IRA. A number of years later, in January 2018, Sinn Féin MP Barry McElduff tweeted a selfie with a loaf of bread of the Kingsmill brand on his head on the day of the anniversary of the massacre. The controversy that ensued revealed the extent to which there can still be either cynicism or denial when it comes to past IRA actions within Republican ranks. While the MP was suspended by the party and eventually tendered his resignation, the fact that he explained that this was a coincidence and not meant to cause any harm shows either that the party has some way to go before ensuring that its public representatives are properly informed, or that they underestimate, or even fail to comprehend, the hurt that IRA actions cause and continue to cause. To some extent, this controversy is akin to the one that arose in November 2020 when a Sinn Féin TD tweeted about the 1979 Warrenpoint attack: 'the 2 IRA operations that taught the elite of d[sic] British army and the establishment the cost of occupying Ireland. Pity for everyone they were such slow learners' (*IT*, 30/11/20; see chapter 3).

The question of whether the IRA was sectarian is not one that is raised by Republicans, who explained attacks on civilians as mistakes or operations that went wrong throughout the conflict. This was the case regarding the Enniskillen bombing, which killed eleven people (all Protestant) on 11 November 1989 at a First World War commemoration, and which was seen by some as deliberately targeting Protestants, since those who remember the First World War were, until recently, mainly from the Protestant community. White's research posits that the operation deviated from the strategy that the IRA had put in place in the late 1970s and that sought to minimise civilian casualties (White, 1997, 41). In general, Republicans explained actions that targeted Protestants as retaliations for Loyalist attacks. White concludes that the IRA killed Protestant civilians, particularly in the years 1975–1976 which account for almost one third of all Protestants killed by the IRA, but explains this by a cycle of tit-for-tat killings and concludes that 'it is perhaps best to view the IRA as a non-sectarian organization that, when they so desire, can and will strike out at the Protestant community in Northern Ireland' (White, 1997, 48). Writing on the nature of the violence during the Troubles, Matthew Lewis and Shaun McDaid convincingly conclude that it is 'best understood as functionally sectarian', inasmuch as it was not directed at the Protestant community because they were Protestants (Lewis & McDaid, 2017, 641). While there is no doubt that a number of operations can be considered sectarian, they find no evidence to support the argument that the IRA campaign amounted to ethnic cleansing.

Reconciliation and 'uncomfortable conversations'

Facing the past requires courage. This is something that Sinn Féin leaders have been repeating over the years, and is a process that they claim to have embarked upon. However, the concept of reconciliation raises many questions that concern not only the participants (who should reconcile with whom) but the process (how should this be achieved) and, even more importantly, the political agenda and the goals that it serves. At the heart of the process are the victims. However, identifying that group proved divisive, before and after the GFA. The first report on the issue, chaired by Kenneth Bloomfield in 1997, gave a far-reaching and inclusive definition: 'the surviving injured and those who care for them, together with those close relatives who mourn their dead' (Bloomfield, 1998, 14). But Unionists felt uncomfortable about granting this status to the dead and injured who had been members of, or had been affiliated to, paramilitary organisations, as they considered them perpetrators and thus could not be seen as victims. This soured the debate in the build-up to the Agreement and in the years that followed, and to this day there is no consensus on the issue. Unionists still talk of 'innocent victims', which implies that they are still processing a hierarchy, thus politicising the debate on suffering and engaging in what has been called a 'war by other means' (Smyth, 2009, 36), which opposes Nationalist and Unionist approaches to victimhood. Such a hierarchy raises many questions, as it conjures up the concept of 'guilty perpetrator' which blames 'them' and exonerates 'us', and that of 'culpable victims', implying that some individuals have contributed to their own victimisation and thus cannot be innocent (Hearty, 2016). Interestingly, the IRA also applied a degree of hierarchy to its victims, when it apologised only to the 'non-combatants' whom it had killed, implying that those it had targeted for being members of the British Army or the security forces had somehow deserved their fate.

Sinn Féin's concept of reconciliation is closely tied to that of unification. In its electoral manifestos, both tend to be presented in the same paragraph and the link between the two is taken for granted: people from both sides of the divide, from both sides of the island, and from both sides of the Irish Sea, need to embark on a reconciliation process. Thus, its 2016 policy document, published in the context of the centenary of the Easter Rising, stated: 'Ending partition and engaging with its impact, legacy and aftermath, is vital if we are to deal with the past and build an agreed and reconciled future' (Sinn Féin, 2016, 2). However, making reconciliation conditional upon the end of partition is problematic. Reunification is still such a divisive prospect that it can hardly constitute a platform on the basis of which to reach out to the other community. Thus, by positing reconciliation as a national effort, Sinn Féin tends to embrace a somewhat vague definition of the concept, extending the responsibility to all, including civil society, and blurring the lines as to what positions need to be shifted, what amends need to be made. There is a risk in such an approach that the responsibility of Republicans could be diluted. Furthermore, reconciliation is not a neutral process, as its approach is influenced by what the different parties bring to the table. As has been argued, it is 'not so much about the past but about ideological reframing(s)' (McGrattan, 2016, 61). More particularly, in the case of Sinn Féin, reconciliation is part of a political programme, an agenda that is embedded in its manifestos. Hopkins further argues that it has become a strategy 'in pursuit of the same goal that violence had manifestly failed to achieve' (Hopkins, 2015, 87).

In order to show leadership in that area, *An Phoblacht* ran a special series of articles called 'uncomfortable conversations' from 2012 to 2017, which were aimed at discussing sensitive and divisive issues concerning the past and the manner in which they should be addressed. The column was open to anyone who wanted to contribute to these 'conversations', and although it was dominated by Republicans, it was also a forum where academic and some Unionist voices were heard. The series gave an insight into how Republicans defined reconciliation and the process that made it possible, but also identified the numerous unresolved issues that still needed discussing.

Declan Kearney, chairman of the party and in charge of reconciliation, was the driving force behind the conversations, and took the lead by publishing an article in which he defined the concept and outlined what was required to achieve it. He explained that 'A deep suspicion remains within unionist communities towards republicans due to the legacy of the armed struggle. Real hurt exists on all sides' (*AP*, 13/8/12), and then outlined the conditions under which reconciliation could take place. At the core of the process was engagement with Unionists, but this was predicated on a number of ground rules. First, it could not become 'a strategy to make unionists into republicans'. Secondly, it was essential to address 'legacy issues and continued suspicion within the wider unionist and Protestant community', and all participants needed to embark upon an introspective process where collective guilt should be admitted. Finally, all sides had to be prepared to listen, and to 'persuade and be persuaded'. However, these efforts had a final goal, and that in itself went against all these ground rules. 'The process of uniting Ireland will be built on increased understanding and mutual respect by reaching out, healing differences, and creating trust with unionists and Protestants' (*AP*, 13/8/12). In some ways, this was the major conundrum that Kearney both identified and avoided. If reconciliation was ultimately about reuniting Ireland, then the basis upon which Unionists would engage with the process was skewed from the outset, and it is difficult to see how they would endorse such a process. A study concluded that the initiative was predicated on those participating having previously engaged with the goals that Sinn Féin had set itself in the process, and observed that the supposed responsibility of 'political Unionism' to engage in the reconciliation agenda is interpreted by most Unionists as an ultimatum, rather than an authentic move towards negotiation, in which 'the *outcome* of the process is uncertain when the protagonists agree to enter into this dialogue' (Hopkins, 2015, 88).

Kearney identified a major stumbling block to this process: the reluctance on the part of Unionists to admit to their share of responsibility in the conflict. 'Political unionism [...] insists that the legacy of our past conflict poses questions only for republicans. It chooses to ignore the origins of the conflict or the roles and actions of the British State, their agencies and of unionism itself in our conflict'. In this narrative, Republicans consider that they are making a greater effort to show their good will. The meeting between the Queen and McGuinness in June 2012, for instance, was hailed as a symbolic moment that showed the party's genuine commitment to reaching out to Unionism. Kearney saw it as a 'huge gesture of reconciliation and friendship from republicans to unionist and Protestant people who owe allegiance to the English monarchy', calling it a 'Mandela moment' (*AP*, 10/04/14). Somewhat naively perhaps, McGuinness himself hoped that this encounter would convince Unionists of the fact that Sinn Féin was genuinely reaching out to them.

However, symbolic gestures are not in themselves sufficient to assuage Unionist suspicions about Sinn Féin's reconciliation agenda. The DUP 2019 manifesto accused Sinn Féin of being 'partial' in its approach to legacy issues, and urged the government to 'ensure terrorists are pursued, with full police powers to conduct effective and comprehensive investigations and arrest suspects. We will do everything we can to assist innocent victims to obtain a measure of justice' (DUP, 2019, 23). It is not only the language used by both parties that is entirely contradictory, it is also the concrete proposals that they put forward. The DUP suggests for instance that Northern Ireland host the annual event for the armed forces, in direct contrast with Sinn Féin's proposed 'Day of Reconciliation that reflects different loyalties but which signals a commitment to building a better future' (Sinn Féin, 2016, 14).

Unionists have also, on occasion, expressed frustration and anger at what they see as the belittling of their identity. Leo Varadkar's reassurance during the Brexit debate that 'The queen will still be the queen, the pound will still be the pound, people will still post letters in Royal Mail red letter boxes' (IT, 18/10/19) provoked an angry retort from Nigel Dodds: 'If Leo Varadkar thinks unionism is just about red post boxes then he is either very ill-informed or else just wishes to be offensive' (BT, 18/10/19). Moreover, the perception that the peace process was weighed in favour of Nationalists, something Republicans would entirely disagree with, is still vivid in some Unionist quarters, the episode of the flags dispute being a good case in point. In December 2012, a section of the Unionist community protested, in some instances forcefully, against the decision of Belfast City Council to fly the Union Jack only on designated dates, in line with the practice in the rest of the UK. Unionists were outraged at a decision seen as an erosion of their identity and of their right to express it. For Republicans, this showed how much Unionists were still clinging to 'the ideology of dominance, a one-party state and one community identity and ethos. It harks back to days that are gone forever' (*AP*, 03/02/13). Other observers would contend, however, that the flags protests were rooted in Loyalist working-class neighbourhoods, where discontent and alienation from the peace process are more pronounced, while most of the political leadership within Unionism looked at the protests from the side-lines (Guelke, 2014, 147). More generally, however, this episode demonstrated the extent to which positions were still entrenched and the importance of time as a factor to be taken into account when addressing even what are perceived by some as symbolic changes. As Dr Heather Morris, President of the Methodist Church, asked in the column of *AP*, the decision to only fly the Union Jack on designated days 'was in accordance with the democratic process, it was folks' right to vote that way, but in terms of the big picture and a shared future was it wise? Would it have been better to bear the cost of holding back that decision?' (*AP*, 31/03/13).

Kearney's 'conversations' initiative produced interesting outcomes. Conferences that gave academics and loyalists the opportunity to share a platform with Republicans were organised, as was the conference named 'Belfast, a City of Equals' which took place in 2013. A relative of two of the victims of the 1993 Shankill bombing and the PSNI Chief Constable also contributed to the newspaper debate. Dawn Purvis, leader of the Progressive Unionist Party since 2011, quoted the succinct assessment of the former leader David Ervine: 'You're going nowhere without me and I am going nowhere without you. The sooner we face that reality the more we can concentrate on building a better future for everyone in this society' (*AP*, 01/09/14). This initiative, according to former Alliance Party leader John Alderdice, thus helped those involved to realise that 'the way forward will require challenging the narratives and attitudes within our own communities about how we leave behind these aspects of our culture and identity' (*AP*, 02/03/15).

The manner in which to address the legacy of the conflict remains one of the thorniest issues in Northern Ireland. Indeed, one of the omissions of the GFA was that while it dedicated a section to reconciliation, it did not identify the mechanisms through which this might be achieved. Several attempts have been made in recent years to put in place a specific course of action to deal with contentious issues such as parades or flags and emblems. But the most difficult question remains that of victims. There are a high number of Trouble-related deaths that are still either unsolved or problematic, which the Historical Enquiries Team, set up in 2006 as part of the PSNI, was tasked with re-examining. However, agreeing on the cases that would need to be investigated proved controversial. Initially, the incidents involving the security forces had been left out, and the number of cases to be investigated was estimated at 1,800, but under pressure from non-governmental organisations (NGOs) and political parties, this was modified to include killings perpetrated by all, as well as cases with insecure convictions (Lundy, 2009, 121), leading to a total of 3,268 unsolved deaths (NIHRC, 2013, 11). This is a high proportion of the 3,600 total Trouble-related deaths, which is the figure most commonly quoted (Mesev et al., 2009, 894). Such cases include the Enniskillen bombing, which killed 11 people in 1987, but for which no conviction was ever pronounced, as well as the Miami Showband and the Kingsmill killings, but also individual deaths. According to a 2018 assessment, the PSNI caseload of unsolved deaths amounted to 1,186, of which 45.5% were attributed to republican paramilitaries, 23% to Loyalist paramilitaries, and 28.5% to the security forces (*The Detail*, 09/04/2018).

The manner in which these legacy issues ought to be approached is contentious. The 2009 report of the consultative group chaired by Robin Eames and Denis Bradley, respectively former Church of Ireland Archbishop of Armagh and former Vice-Chair of the Northern Ireland Policing Board, generated fierce debate. It focused largely on its two main recommendations: the establishment of a legacy commission to look into some of the killings which occurred during the conflict, and £12,000 compensation for victims of killings (CGP, 2009). The furore over the latter was mainly due to the fact that there was no distinction between victims, whether they had been killed by paramilitaries or by the security forces, while the legacy commission was considered too close to a truth recovery process for events that had occurred in a relatively recent past (Hancock, 2012). In 2013, the Northern Ireland Executive published an ambitious plan of action: *Together: Building a United Community* (Belfast, 2013) aimed at introducing a new good relations paradigm. US Senator Richard Haass and Dr Megan O'Sullivan, former Deputy National Security Advisor for Iraq and Afghanistan, agreed to facilitate a negotiation process, in an effort to find a consensus among the five major political parties in Northern Ireland (DUP, Sinn Féin, UUP, SDLP, Alliance) (interview with Richard Haass, *Foreign Affairs*, 29/01/14).[8] However, in spite of intense negotiations, and in the midst of the flags dispute, the Proposed Agreement of 31 December 2013 was rejected by three of the parties – the DUP, the UUP and the Alliance Party. The Stormont House Agreement, reached on 23 December 2014, again provided for measures to deal with legacy issues: a Historical Investigations Unit, which would look at outstanding cases, an Independent Commission on Information Retrieval, which would give victims and survivors access to information on the loss of their loved ones, and an Oral Archive for people to share their experiences and narratives. As the Community Relations Council's Fifth report remarked, The *Fresh Start Agreement* of 2015 reaffirmed the governments' commitment to those mechanisms, but as there were no specific ways in which to implement them, they remained aspirational (Gray et al., 2018, 75). The actual work was delayed due to the ongoing opposition from the main Unionist organisations to a process which they feared would inevitably be biased against the security forces. Indeed, Prime Minister Theresa May shared those concerns and explained in May 2018 that 'the only people being investigated for these issues are those in our armed forces or those who served in law enforcement in Northern Ireland ... That is patently unfair. Terrorists are not being investigated' BBC, 09/05/18). To this was added the debate as to whether a statute of limitation should apply and, if so, whether it should include former paramilitaries as well as security personnel, which would, in effect, amount to an amnesty. Unionists were fiercely opposed to the idea, as they do not consider that all perpetrators have the same rights and duties. But to Sinn Féin's Linda Dillon, spokesperson for legacy issues, 'the reality is that British state forces killed people here and somebody has to be answerable', adding that 'there were hundreds of people killed in collusion with the state forces, but nobody has been answerable for that. That's the difference, where there was evidence against Republicans, you can be damn sure those republicans went to jail' (Dillon, interview, September 2020). Collusion is still, indeed, an unresolved issue. For some, the issue has been used by republicans to further their agenda, while the instances of collusion between republican informants and the British security forces has not led to calls for investigation (Cochrane, 2013). Nevertheless, the Pat Finucane case,[9] possibly the most famous, and illustrative, example of the debate generated by collusion, also raises a number of wider questions: 'how the rule of law was and is implemented in Northern Ireland, how far up the chain of command collusion went, and how to address the ghosts of the North's past, which continue to haunt its future' (*IT*, 30/11/20). For Michelle O'Neill, the British rejection of a public enquiry in November 2020, which has been the family's and supporters' main demand, was a 'manoeuvre to deny accountability and facilitate impunity for state actors particularly when the evidence speaks to an overarching state conspiracy in the murder of Pat Finucane' (PR, 30/11/20).

Sinn Féin has been consistent in its approach to legacy issues, calling for a truth recovery mechanism to be put in place as 'the best way to approach the past' (Sinn Féin, 2016, 7). However, there is little appetite amongst Unionists for such a process, as they fear that it would be used mainly to investigate deaths perpetrated by the security forces. In the eyes of Unionists, these deaths cannot be treated in the same manner as those for which paramilitaries are responsible, since their actions were carried out in the name of the State and with the legitimacy afforded by the institutions to which they belonged. Sinn Féin MLA Linda Dillon regrets that the 'Truth and reconciliation process did not go ahead. That's where we wanted to go. And that was our position for a number of years. We pushed hard on that. And we just couldn't get anybody else to go down that route' (Dillon, interview, September 2020). The fault line between Sinn Féin on one side, and the Unionists and British government on the other, was illustrated by the controversy that followed an exchange in Westminster between then Secretary of State for Northern Ireland Karen Bradley and a DUP

MP in 2019. Responding to the MPs' question on legacy issues, Bradley stated that

> over 90 per cent of the killings during the Troubles were at the hands of terrorists, every single one of those was a crime. The fewer than 10 per cent that were at the hands of the military and police were not crimes. They were people acting under orders and under instruction and fulfilling their duty in a dignified and appropriate way. (*IT*, 6/3/19)

Bradley subsequently apologised, given the magnitude of the controversy that her comments generated. However, what this assessment revealed was the gulf that still existed between the two sides on the manner in which victims are considered, which is closely linked to the reasons for the violence and its legitimacy.

Sinn Féin remains highly critical of the British government's approach. According to Linda Dillon, 'they have reneged on everything that they have ever agreed to in relation to legacy'. She referred to the mechanisms agreed by all that 'would have led us to a point where we could have really started the reconciliation process' (Dillon, interview, September 2020). Indeed, the British government has moved away from the initial approach of the Stormont House Agreement, pledging to end the 'cycle of reinvestigations into the Troubles in Northern Ireland that has failed victims and [British Army] veterans alike' (*IT*, 30/11/20). This has been compounded by the legislation on the compensation scheme for the victims of the Troubles introduced by the Secretary of State in January 2020 and originally scheduled to be operational from May 2020. However, its implementation was delayed following a dispute over whether Westminster or Stormont should pay the bill, estimated at £100 million. The Executive failed to nominate a Department that would take responsibility for implementing the scheme, generating delays for the victims themselves. The dispute opened another rift, this more fundamental, between the two main coalition partners – the DUP and Sinn Féin – which centred around the clause that defined the eligibility criteria, and that included those who had been injured 'through no fault of their own' but not those who had been convicted of terrorist offences. This, in Mary Lou McDonald's opinion, amounted to excluding many Nationalists. Some of the victims, who had in some cases been waiting for compensation for decades, had little patience for the arguments made by both sides and took their case to the Northern Ireland High Court, which ruled that the Executive was to meet its obligation and nominate a Department that would take responsibility for implementing the scheme. Michelle O'Neill relented, but restated her party's belief that 'the policy intent was and remains to create a hierarchy of victims, and reinforce the British state narrative around the conflict', while Arlene Foster tweeted that it was '[n]ow time for Sinn Fein to prioritise innocent victims rather than bombers' (RTÉ, 21/08/20). Both comments encapsulate the stalemate in which the two coalition partners in the Executive are locked, and which it does not seem possible to break, for the time being at least.

From the start of the peace process, Sinn Féin has remained steadfastly loyal to its former ally, the IRA.

However, the narrative that it has developed is complex and its proponents are not simply the guardians of the IRA temple. They have strived to ensure that the memory of the IRA lives on, but that it adapts to the political progress made by the party. This means both promoting a narrative that sheds a positive light on the paramilitary organisation, and downplaying actual events, controversies and operations which could tarnish the organisation, focusing instead on individuals. This Sinn Féin does through the numerous commemorations and celebrations organised throughout the year, which serve both as a gathering point for members and sympathisers, and as a way to ensure that meaning is given to thirty years of conflict. With time, however, the narrative is morphing and the ultimate goal could be, once living memory has faded, to only remember the IRA in the same manner as the 'old IRA' was celebrated: as a force for progress, using violence as an inevitable evil. Undoubtedly, this creates tensions with most of its political opponents and could ultimately be seen as damaging the party's strategy on reconciliation and reunification. But as Danny Morrison once said about the 'Armalite and ballot box' strategy, 'all parties have their contradictions. We can live with it'.

3

The radical, left-wing party

It's a good time to be a left Republican. (Ó Broin, interview, August 2020)

Sinn Féin presents itself as a progressive, left-wing party. In the words of Dublin Mid-West TD Eoin Ó Broin:

if you look at the broad party platform, whether that is on housing, health, childcare, pensions, community developments, there is a very clear and strong and positive radical left programme in terms of the wealth distribution, universal health public policies and addressing inequalities and unfairness in Irish society. (Ó Broin, interview, August 2020)

This view is confirmed by Dublin South central TD Aengus Ó Snodaigh, although he is more guarded as to the extent of the radicalism of the party: 'I'm proud to be left and proud to be radical, but others would be presumed to be more radical. I'm happy where the party is and that's where I hope it stays without becoming too unreasonable. When that's too far, you're out of touch with people, you might want to go down that road, but you can't isolate yourself from the people and from your base' (Ó Snodaigh, interview, August 2020).

Sinn Féin was not always that comfortable with this markedly left-wing identity. For most of the twentieth century, its relationship with socialism was conflicted. However, its electoral engagement in the early 1980s translated into advances in the most economically disadvantaged areas in Northern Ireland, which in turn generated a major ideological shift. Progressively, the party managed to make its policies on social issues one of its trademarks. The days when its proposals were considered far-fetched and unrealistic are over, as the party has seen the rise among its ranks of articulate and competent policy-makers. Finance spokesperson Pearse Doherty's pre-budget submissions were once decried as 'Shinnernomics'. But the conservative *Sunday Independent* described him, as early as 2012, as 'one to watch right now, and in the future', one whose 'persistent and intelligent questioning' made him into 'a significant thorn in the Government's side' (24/06/12). His analysis is now sought by shows such as the *Irish Times* weekly podcast 'Inside Business'.[1] The party's policy on housing, put together by Eoin Ó Broin, is largely seen as both novel and feasible. For experts such as Emeritus Professor Tony Fahey, Ó Broin's book *Home* (2019) showed an approach 'with policy experience and a left-wing perspective, but with no simple solutions' (*IT*, 06/09/19).

Undoubtedly, the manner in which Sinn Féin has strategised its left-wing approach has been long and painstaking, as it has had to tread carefully along a path on which so many other versions of Sinn Féin had travelled and stumbled. The party underwent a number of splits, most notably the 1970 division between Officials and Provisionals. In the early years of the twenty-first century, however, Eoin Ó Broin laid out the political orientations of the party, advocating an approach 'informed by the radicalism of the New Left, anti-imperialism, feminism, ecologism and other popular movements' (Ó Broin, 2009. 3). Contradicting the predictions of those who viewed this strategy as 'unlikely to be adopted by a party leadership that has firmly placed itself in the mainstream and seems unwilling or unable to move from that cherished centre ground' (Bean et al., 2010, 139), it would seem that this vision did prevail. Sinn Féin's increased focus on societal issues – translating into: an active involvement in the Marriage Equality and Repeal the Eighth referenda; its prioritising of economic policies on housing and health; its success at broadening its appeal to the middle classes and younger generations; its grassroots approach to activism and its engagement with social media – all combined to build a new image, that of an engaged, energetic and forward-looking party, while not reneging on its ultimate goal, Irish unity.

Re-branding the party

Sinn Féin has successfully transitioned from being mainly identified with self-determination and national unity to radical, left-wing orientations. While it has always claimed to defend the interests of the most vulnerable sections of the population, for decades its discourse was mainly targeted at the Nationalist community in Northern Ireland, and particularly the working-class areas, which have constituted the bedrock of republicanism. Being grounded in these communities certainly contributed to making the transition from a Nationalist to a left-wing discourse smoother. In contrast, the process of finding a constituency that would identify with its discourse in the Republic was not as straightforward. No matter how strong its engagement in social issues, it was perceived as prioritising partition, which debate only started gaining traction in Irish public discourse from the mid-2010s.[2] This has remained central to Sinn Féin's discourse, which inextricably links Irish unity and social progress, but the party has successfully demonstrated how this can be operationalised and strategised. In order to convince the electorate of this dual approach, Sinn Féin gradually anchored its policy programmes around a dual axis, that of social progressivism and a strong advocacy for state intervention in economic affairs, without deviating from its main objective.

On the eve of the 1980–1981 hunger strikes and of the rise to leadership positions within Sinn Féin of a new generation of young Northerners, a discourse that put more emphasis on the social class dimension of the conflict emerged. The political situation was increasingly analysed in terms of an oppressed proletariat (both Catholic and Protestant) and the 'establishment' (British, Unionist, capitalist). The entry of Sinn Féin into electoral politics was thus accompanied by a deliberate left-wing turn, as the appeal to the voters would no longer be focused on the national question. As such, the eulogy that Owen Carron[3] made at Bobby Sands' funeral left no doubt as to how Sinn Féin would build on this episode of recent Republican history and set the tone for the place that the party intended to occupy on the Irish political scene:

> Bobby Sands is a symbol of hope for the unemployed, for the poor and oppressed, for the homeless, for those divided by partition, for those trying to unite our people. He symbolises a new beginning and I recall the words of his manifesto to the Protestant people: 'The Protestant people have nothing to fear from me.' They too have their part to play in building a new future, a new Ireland. (AP, 09/05/81)

This was also how Sinn Fein chose to woo voters in the Republic, when it first decided to test the electoral waters in the 1982 general election.[4] Its manifesto was 'directed to the under-privileged, the young, the low-paid worker, the small farmer, the women, the young, and to the unemployed – to all the victims of imperialist and native capitalist oppression' (AP, 09/02/82). This did not pay off immediately, as it would take another fifteen years for one of its candidates to be elected to the Dáil.[5] And while that type of rhetoric was sufficiently broad to be consensual within the movement, its leaders were careful not to brand too precisely this anti-imperialistic, anti-capitalist and pro-proletarian focus. Indeed, there was very little appetite in the 1980s and early 1990s for a left-wing discourse on either sides of the island. This was a niche that Sinn Féin set itself to occupy, but it was careful to do so without antagonising its basic constituency.

Adams reassured his supporters in 1986 that there would be no major departure from republican priorities: 'I don't think that socialism is on the agenda at this stage, except for political activists on the left. What's on the agenda now is an end to partition. You won't get near socialism until you have national independence. It's a prerequisite' (*IT*, 10/12/86). Yet, a few years later, a policy document presented a 'visionary and credible alternative based on a "decentralised socialism" that would be realistic, flexible and adapted to the needs of the Irish people' (Sinn Féin, c. 1994, 4).

At the turn of the twenty-first century, Sinn Féin started to elaborate a suite of policy programmes that covered previously unexplored grounds, shedding language that no longer resonated with the public at large. While it still saw its aim as achieving a '32-county democratic socialist republic', this type of rhetoric was progressively expunged from its documents. In fact, the word 'socialist' last featured in a 2011 manifesto. Indeed, from the early 2000s, Sinn Féin fully endorsed its left-wing orientations. This ideological trajectory didn't take place in a vacuum, but was grounded in a context conducive to the rise of a left–right axis in the politics of the Irish Republic. Until then, the consensual analysis was that in terms of traditional right–left divisions, Ireland was the 'odd one out', as 'party competition throughout the twentieth century, famously, did not pivot on a left–right axis but between two centre-right parties' (McElroy, 2017, 1). However, by the mid-2010s, that division had entered the political culture. A study exploring the ability of voters to place Irish parties on the general left–right dimension found the electorate was able 'to distinguish parties from each other in terms of their left–right placement' (McElroy, 2017, 7), which represented a departure from what was considered traditional politics until then. On a left–right scale of 0 to 10, Sinn Féin was positioned at 2.82, although 28% of respondents could not place Sinn Féin on the spectrum at all (McElroy, 2017, 5).

Behind this repositioning of the Irish political system is undoubtedly the 2008 financial crisis, during which Ireland experienced levels of austerity unknown in most other EU countries, as well as soaring rates of unemployment. The debt to GDP ratio rose from 32% in 2007 to 97% by the end of 2010, and general government debt increased by 320% over the same period. Unemployment jumped from 4.6% in 2007 to 14.2% in June 2011 (Kinsella, 2012, 224). This was accompanied by a series of cutbacks in the welfare system, such as the universal child benefit, the jobseeker's allowance for the young unemployed, and by increases in taxation (public sector pension levy, cuts to income tax credits, introduction of a universal social charge, and cuts in public service pay) (Savage et al., 2019). Austerity measures spearheaded the rise of a radical left-wing discourse, mainly through the voice of parties such as People Before Profit[6] who, while its capacity to rally voters around its candidates remains low (its vote went from 1% in 2011 to 3.9% in 2016 and 2.6% in 2020), was nevertheless able to channel some of the popular discontent which escalated with the announcement in 2010 that water charges, dropped in 1978, were to be reintroduced. As a result, Ireland experienced unprecedented levels of civil resistance, and in some cases, disobedience (Trommer, 2019).[7] Thousands of people took to the streets, eventually succeeding in meeting their objective, the repeal of the water charges, formally dropped in April 2017 (IT, 13/04/17).

The water charges episode illustrated the predicament in which Sinn Féin found itself. Indeed, while its radical left-wing policy naturally placed the party on the side of the protesters, it was outflanked on its left by those who had called for the non-payment of the charges, a tactic which Sinn Féin did not endorse officially, with several leaders stating that they would pay the charges. The issue seemed to divide the party itself, and generated a level of confusion as to what the actual line was. This came to a head during the October 2014 by-election in Dublin West, where the Socialist Party candidate Paul Murphy, running under the banner of the Anti-Austerity Alliance, defeated the Sinn Féin candidate Cathal King.[8] Subsequently, following a protest held on 1 November 2014, which was attended by 'tens of thousands' (IT, 01/11/14), McDonald announced that she would not pay the tax. The episode raised interesting questions about the direction that Sinn Féin was planning to take. By refusing initially to place themselves outside the law, the leadership of the party were signalling that their bid for government was serious and thus that Sinn Féin was a trustworthy party. However, for those to its left, this was an admission of weakness and cast a shadow over its radical edge. The Socialist

Party online magazine fustigated Sinn Féin's 'weak' opposition to and then 'back-pedalling' on the payment of
water charges (18/04/15). The episode thus highlighted
the complexity of Sinn Féin's relationship with the radical left. A 2017 study on the water charges movement
listed the three main issues of friction between the two.
First was the age-old tension between Nationalism and
left-wing politics, which James Connolly had confronted
almost a century beforehand (Chilton, 2015). Then came
the fact that Sinn Féin's ministers in Northern Ireland
had, in the view of their critics, implemented austerity
politics, and this, combined with the fact that they were
prepared to go into government with Fianna Fáil, dented
their credibility. But perhaps more damning of all three
criticisms, as it pointed to the lack of clarity of Sinn
Féin's political direction, was the fact that these critics saw the party's 'future political direction – leftwards
or rightwards – as being as yet undecided' (Dunphy,
2017, 279).

The equality agenda

These critical voices have yet to pose a substantial challenge to Sinn Féin. One of the issues with which the
radical left is confronted is the fragmentation of its ranks
and representatives. Meanwhile, Sinn Féin has shown
its capacity to strengthen its image as a left-wing alternative, although the direction that it takes on specific
issues is not always clear. One of the key elements that
explains its success was the articulation of a strategy that

would be both inclusive and consensual. The peace process brought to the fore a new language centred around a key concept: equality. Its 2003 policy document *No Right Turn* featured terms such as parity of esteem, consent and equality, becoming the paradigm within which the discourse was constructed: 'Equality must be the cornerstone of our society and our economy. People should be treated as citizens with rights, not just consumers with more or less spending power'. In contrast, right-wing policies were equivalent to survival of the fittest, [...] individualism and private enterprise' which saw 'true equality for all as a threat' (2003). Equality encapsulated what Sinn Féin stood for, on both sides of the border – a concept that made it possible to federate constituencies while bringing some texture to its United Ireland objective. This became the axis around which all policy programmes would pivot. This was more than a rhetorical tool, it was an ideological statement which was adapted to all areas of social policy, with the multiplication of slogans and catchphrases such as 'Equal rights for Irish speakers', 'For a future of equals', 'Rights for all', 'Equality, diversity, solidarity'. On a par with economic proposals, Sinn Féin put social and cultural rights at the top of its agenda, with a focus on gender and LGBT (Lesbian, Gay, Bisexual and Transgender) rights and anti-racism. But maintaining a coherent line sometimes proved problematic. The stark reality is that the movement and the electorate in general might not always have been fully behind radical approaches to societal issues. Three issues in particular illustrate the tension between policy programmes and reality on the ground: marriage equality, abortion and immigration. While the first was, overall, unproblematic, the other two proved more challenging for the party to navigate.

The 2015 Marriage Equality referendum was a watershed moment in the recent history of the Republic of Ireland,[9] with 62.07% of the population voting in favour of amending the constitution to allow for same-sex marriage. Ireland thus became the first country in the world to approve of such a measure by popular vote. Amongst the most remarkable features of the referendum were the alignment of all political parties on the Yes side, and a 'heavily grassroots oriented' campaign (Murphy, 2016, 320). On the day of the results, Gerry Adams tweeted a selfie of himself with drag queen Panti Bliss, AKA Rory O'Neill, the 'accidental activist of Ireland' (*NY Times*, 19/08/15). The tweet was qualified by the *Irish Independent* as an 'embarrassing' moment for the leader of Sinn Féin (*II*, 20/10/15), and the *Guardian* commented: 'RTÉ is interviewing both Gerry Adams and drag queen Panti Bliss. Now that's progress' (23/05/15). Yet, Sinn Féin's engagement with LGBT issues was nothing new. *Moving On: A Policy for Lesbian, Gay and Bi-Sexual Equality*, published in the early 2000s, explained that 'Republicans are only too well aware of what it means to be treated as second-class citizens' (1).[10] The policy document included a set of demands (which fell short of marriage equality) but also, interestingly, a number of measures to educate its own members and raise awareness at all levels of the party on LGBT issues and on the fight against homophobia. The theme of LGBT equality was then further developed in its 2007 manifestos,[11] demanding the introduction of same-sex marriage and the right to adopt 'in the same manner as heterosexual couples' (Sinn Féin Manifesto and Women's Manifesto, 2007, 63, 31). It was only four year later that the Labour Party made a similar demand in its 2011 manifesto.

Three years after the Marriage Equality referendum came the campaign to Repeal the Eighth amendment,[12] which proved more sensitive for the party, as this had been a divisive issue for a number of years. Sinn Féin had been well ahead of most of its counterparts on the issue of women's rights, with the creation in the early 1980s of a women's department. This was a site of resistance that allowed the elaboration of a feminist discourse and reflection on the Troubles, but also on the movement itself. It thus became a 'potent and radical political force', led not by the leadership, but by the women themselves (Gilmartin, 2017, 375). Sinn Féin became the first party in Ireland to adopt a pro-choice stance on the issue of abortion in 1985, although the vote was reversed the following year due to the controversy that it generated among its own members.[13] The women's department was replaced in the mid-1990s by an equality department and its radicalism was diluted, as the movement was 'shifting towards a more institutional path and so, grassroots activism was something that required tempering and refinement to fit in with the new institutional departure' (Gilmartin, 2017, 283). While the movement actively promoted women within the organisation, nominating them to top positions (Bairbre de Brún was the minister for Health in the very first Northern Ireland Executive, from 1999 to 2002, and a policy of quotas was put in place for elections), the implementation of such measures did not produce as radical a change as expected. 'The party has been more committed than others to supporting the use of equality guarantees and supportive actions to increase women's presence in internal leadership positions. Yet its record in electoral politics has been more rhetorical, stating support for affirmative actions, but showing very little evidence of implementing such strategies' (Buckley, 2013, 352).

Sinn Féin's position on abortion was, in its 2016 manifesto, limited to specific circumstances. It thus aimed to 'legislate for a referendum to repeal the Eighth Amendment in order to provide for a woman to seek a termination of a pregnancy where her life is at risk or in grave danger, and in cases of rape or incest as well as in cases of fatal foetal abnormalities'. In line with this, the party campaigned strongly for the repeal of the Eighth Amendment, as, according to McDonald, this was 'a relic of an Ireland of the past. Yet, it restricts the rights of women in the here and now and affects our future in such a profound way. It has to go' (PR, 09/3/18). Labour, People Before Profit, the Social Democrats and the Greens were the only parties to support the introduction of legislation that would allow abortion for the first twelve weeks. Sinn Féin did not change its position until after the referendum, as any new stance needed to be adopted by the party convention (Ard Fheis), which introduced, in June 2018, the right for women to access abortions 'within a limited gestational period' (BBC, 16/06/18). The party does not allow a vote of conscience on the issue, contrary to Fine Gael and Fianna Fáil, which led to some internal turmoil and the eventual loss of two TDs. Offaly TD Carol Nolan, who had been suspended in March 2018 for three months for refusing to vote for a bill that would allow legislation on the subject (which was passed by 100 to 32 votes), resigned in 2018 when the party endorsed the right to choose. Peadar Tóibín also left the party and founded his own organisation, Aontú (see chapter 1).

In Northern Ireland, advances on reproductive and LGBT rights have been much slower, as SDLP Claire Hanna acknowledged: 'We are 5 years behind' (public debate, 12/11/20).[14] Gender and LGBT issues were inextricably tied to the conflict, which slowed down progress on equality. Women tended to be confined to the private space, with the militarised nature of society heightening levels of domestic violence and hindering the fight for reproductive rights (Ashe, 2017). Added to this was the invisibility of women in the political sphere, until the formation of the Women's Coalition in 1996, which gave women a voice throughout the negotiations and an influence on the final outcome of the GFA, but did not necessarily pave the way for their further inclusion. Indeed, some studies have shown that consociationalism[15] is not 'good for women', as it renders them invisible and does not actively promote their place in public life. The post-agreement period has not proved conducive to the advancement of women or LGBT rights, as the fundamental aim of consociationalism is to end violence, not injustice (Taylor, 2009).

Reproductive and LGBT rights have become another major fault line between Nationalists and Unionists, an issue that has been politicised by both sides, with Sinn Féin stating in its 2007 Assembly manifesto that 'The DUP in particular has actively used homophobia for political gain' (47). Both parties have been taking on the role of 'moral guardians' of the LGBT and abortion rights at opposite ends of the spectrum (LSE blog, 20/06/17). The electorate is equally divided along ethno-Nationalist lines, although views are rapidly changing on these matters. The NILT survey asked respondents in 2016 and 2018 to take a stance on the following statement: 'Is it a woman's right to choose whether or not to have not an abortion?' Over these two years, the percentage of those agreeing increased from 63% to 71%. Interestingly, the results per religion show that the difference between Catholics and Protestants is minor, with Catholics moving from to 59% to 70% and Protestants from 63% to 66%. These figures indicate that in 2018, most Northern Ireland parties were out of sync with their electors, including Sinn Féin until it changed its own position.

After failed attempts to legislate in favour of marriage equality[16] and to decriminalise abortion, Northern Ireland was brought in line with other parts of the UK in 2019 with a vote in Westminster. Same-sex marriage was thus made legal by the Northern Ireland (Executive Formation etc.) Act 2019, which also decriminalised abortion.[17] The DUP, which sought to 'Protect Mothers and Unborn Life

Again' (DUP, 2019, 26), introduced a motion in Stormont in June 2020 which sought to ban abortion, particularly in cases of non-fatal foetal abnormality. This was carried by 46 to 40 votes. Sinn Féin had tabled an amendment, supporting the restriction for non-fatal abnormality, thus contradicting the very stance it had taken two years previously, which clearly stated that 'abortion without specific indication should be available through a GP-led service in a clinical context as determined by law and licensing practice for a limited gestational period' (Sinn Féin, Clár, 2018). Mary Lou McDonald tweeted on that occasion that 'Sinn Féin opposes & will vote against the DUP motion this evening. Sinn Féin actively supported #repealedThe8th & the subsequent legislation. Sinn Féin wants those same rights secured for women in the South to be delivered in the North. Nobody left behind'.[18] However, the exact extent of those rights was not clarified by the party, whose position of the termination of pregnancy in the North seemed at odds with views held in the Republic. The episode illustrated the difficulties of being an all-Ireland party and having to contend with different constituencies and membership on issues that are not equally consensual on both sides of the border. Sinn Féin was criticised by the Green Party for political opportunism, but also, and for entirely different reasons, by the SDLP who, through the voice of MLA Dolores Kelly, condemned what was perceived as Sinn Féin's hypocrisy: 'I fail to understand why a so-called republican party supports a British government in determining the right to life of unborn Irish children. It's

a long way from the Proclamation of 1916 which promised to cherish all of the children of the nation equally'
(*IT*, 02/06/20). Amnesty International urged the party to
reverse its position, which, in its view, sent 'a regrettable
message' and called for an end to 'stigma and shame for
all women' (Amnesty International, PR, 02/06/20). Also
worthy of note is the fact that abortion is only mentioned in the 2016 electoral manifesto which pledged to
support the Repeal the Eighth referendum. Undeniably,
there is a level of tension not only within the party, but
between both sides of the border, which translates into
somewhat inconsistent stances and creates confusion as
to where the party actually stands on this issue.

The equality agenda can nevertheless enable Sinn Féin
to transcend its traditional vote base and garner support from quarters who do not traditionally vote for its
candidates. Thus, involvement in the Marriage Equality
and Repeal the Eighth referenda undoubtedly brought
some benefits. These are issues with which Sinn Féin
can hope to build some support among those who do not
vote according to Nationalist/Unionist lines and who are
more liberal in their overall attitudes. Sinn Féin MLA
Caoimhe Archibald sees this as an opportunity that the
party can grasp:

> I think there is a kind of middle ground there that is more
> progressive that we reach out to. Some of the campaigns
> that we were involved in, in the cases around repeal and
> marriage equality, create an opportunity. For example,
> transfers that we may not have gotten in the past that we
> now get. So I think there is a growing middle ground there

that we're reaching out to. So there is the opportunity still
to grow. (Archibald, interview, October 2020).

Indeed, the percentage of those not declaring a religion in
Northern Ireland is increasing and the NILT survey indicates that this constituency's views were overwhelmingly more liberal on the right to choose, with 72% in
favour in 2016 and 88% in 2018. However, capturing and
harnessing this share of the vote is not an easy task. The
University of Liverpool's 2015 general election survey
found that a sizeable section of the under thirties don't
identify along ethno-Nationalist lines, that they are more
'secular minded' but less likely to vote, and that they
have a low interest in politics. Capturing the youth vote –
a cohort with which it successfully made headways in
the Republic of Ireland – is thus fundamental for Sinn
Féin if it wants to progress beyond its current level of
support.

While LGBT and gender issues have been very visible
in public discourse since the start of the 2010s, the topic
of immigration, so prevalent in other EU countries, has
next to no salience in Irish general election campaigns.
However, all parties dedicated a section to the subject
in their 2020 manifestos, containing specific and concrete proposals, with Sinn Féin's being the briefest. The
EU website on integration carried out a comparative
analysis of different parties' commitments. It concluded
that Labour, the Social Democrats, the Green Party and
People Before Profit had the most developed political programmes on migration and integration, with Fianna Fáil

and Fine Gael giving less prominence to the issue. Sinn Féin, for its part, 'offered only a general statement on immigration and committed to introducing laws against hate crimes and access to healthcare for asylum seekers' (EU website on integration, 2020). The first three parties advocated for the extension of voting rights for migrants, the reversal of the 2004 referendum, which restricted the right to citizenship of all children born in Ireland, and the regularisation of undocumented migrants. While Sinn Féin is also committed to these objectives, they did not feature in its programme, which only mentioned the need to end the direct provision system[19] and to introduce hate crime legislation.[20]

However, the party's approach to immigration was more developed at the turn of the century, when it published a comprehensive policy document, *Many Voices One Country*, outlining detailed proposals on anti-racism strategy and immigration goals. The document was far-reaching and contained forward-looking and even avant-garde proposals, which were all-encompassing. Its views on economic migration were progressive, as the party advocated recruitment for labour purposes 'to ensure that potential immigrants from both developing nations and countries of greatest need are given equality in terms of immigrant numbers'. Sinn Féin also has a strong record on the fight against racism. It is credited for having a 'resolute stance against anti-immigrant views' (*IT*, 17/01/20). It called for a No vote in the 2004 citizenship referendum, which amended the constitution in order to put an end to the automatic right to citizenship for all children born in Ireland, and which was approved by a resounding 79.1% of the population. Adams lambasted the poll as making 'a joke of our claim to be Ireland of the welcomes. If it's passed, we will be creating a completely unequal society for future generations' (PR, 31/05/04). Sinn Féin subsequently supported a bill introduced by People Before Profit that 'addresses a major issue of fundamental human rights in respect of allowing these Irish children[21] to remain in Ireland' (DD, 17/01/19). This was in line with the vast majority of its voters (78%), who agreed that anyone born on the island of Ireland should be automatically entitled to Irish citizenship (*The Journal* 18/11/18).[22] Sinn Féin is also on record for its strong opposition to the system of direct provision, and for its call to give the right to vote in general elections to all non-Irish nationals (who can currently only vote in local elections) (Fanning et al., 2007). It endorsed the Migrant Rights Centre's proposal in 2017 to regularise undocumented migrants. The Oireachtas Joint Committee on Justice and Equality, which looked at the system of direct provision and recommended its disbandment, was chaired by Sinn Féin TD Caoimhghín Ó Caoláin.

Perhaps the reason why the 2020 manifesto undermined questions of immigration, considering the party's track record, can be summed up in one word: pragmatism. The shift from an inclusive policy of migration that looks on a par at sending and receiving countries' needs was replaced by an approach which can be considered more instrumentalist and self-serving, one where migrants fill the gaps or shortages in the labour market: 'This system must have regard to how many people are needed to meet shortfalls in the labour market and how many people can be integrated effectively with adequate support and resourcing. Where we do need migrants, such as to fill vacancies in our health system, our migration system should facilitate this'. Equally, the party made it clear that it did not 'want open borders. We believe that all states must manage migration' (70). While no party advocates for open borders, the fact that Sinn Féin was the only one to state this could be interpreted as a tightening of its position on migration, especially in light of the more empathetic approaches taken by the party on questions of asylum.[23] Eoin Ó Broin, however, explains that manifestos cannot fully capture the full range of policies and stances that the party adopts, as they are not 'encyclopaedias' (Ó Broin, interview, August 2020). But while the commitment of the party on the rights of migrants is solid, it would seem that this is not an issue with which it chooses to be closely identified when embarking on an election campaign.

Social engagement

Sinn Féin is a pragmatic party, and is determined to increase its share of the vote. Unsurprisingly, the areas of its manifestos that are most developed are those which will resonate most with electors. Opinion polls since 2016 show that the issues prioritised by voters in the Republic of Ireland are health and housing, with unemployment trailing behind:

Table 1   Issues prioritised by voters in the Republic of Ireland, 2016–2019 (%)

Issue	May 2016		Jan 2017		Nov 2019	
	All	Sinn Féin	All	Sinn Féin	All	Sinn Féin
Health services/ hospitals	68	73	68	71	59	61
Homelessness/ lack of local authority housing	51	59	50	60	66	70
Unemployment	39	46	32	37	22	24

Source: Compilation of *Sunday Times* polls.

Sinn Féin's proposals are based on the observation that the manner in which the wealth of the country is redistributed is fundamentally unfair and benefits the upper strata of society. Thus, in order to restore some balance and to improve the livelihoods of those who are 'left behind', it has put together a number of radical proposals. All have one element in common, in that they place the State at the centre of the redistribution and economic regulation mechanisms. Sinn Féin's approach is thus strongly interventionist. The measures all call for an increased role of the State in public sectors of the economy, and advocate a new taxation system, with the abolition of what are seen as unfair taxes – property and water charges, introduced and partly withdrawn during austerity. Sinn Féin also seeks a major overhaul of the system, which would place a greater taxation onus on higher revenues, through, for instance: the introduction of a third rate of income tax on individual earnings over €100,000; a tax on individual net wealth in excess of €1 million; and the increase of the tax take as a percentage. Obviously, a number of criticisms were voiced, such as that of IBEC (Irish Business and Employers Confederation) who, without directly mentioning Sinn Féin, warned that such proposals 'will undermine the ability of business to create the resources which allow government to provide for society and address the big challenges that lie ahead' (*IT*, 04/02/20). The Chartered Accountants Ireland, while acknowledging that there was 'so much to like' in the manifesto, also warned that the proposals were 'not sustainable. They would bring in additional money in year one, but not in years two, three or four'. Going even further, the criticism pointed to the core ideas (higher taxation on a small proportion of individuals, extensive tax reliefs for cohorts of workers in the lower income brackets, and a significant increase in public sector day-to-day spending) as being no longer valid: 'Ireland has moved on. The Sinn Féin manifesto needs to as well' (Keegan, 2020). Sinn Féin is undeterred and claims that all its proposals have been costed and can be justified. Their 2021 pre-budget submission further developed such proposals, suggesting an injection of additional funding into healthcare, a reversal of the cut in the Pandemic Unemployment Payment (originally €350, but reduced to €300 in September 2020), and a revamping of the taxation system in line with what it had been proposed in February 2020 (Sinn Féin, *Alternative Budget 2021*, 2020).

Health, described as 'one of the key battlegrounds in the election campaign' (*IT*, 06/02/20), was the priority of all parties. Over recent years, the public health care system in Ireland has been noted for its shortcomings, being 'the only western European country without universal access to primary care' (*State of Health in the EU*, 2019, 68). On the eve of the COVID-19 pandemic, medical experts were warning of the imminent crisis, with: hospital bed occupancy up to 95%, the highest in Europe; the ratio of intensive care beds at 5.2 per 100,000 population, against a European average of 11.5; extended waiting times both for consultant appointments and in Emergency Rooms (*IE*, 12/02/20). Health is an ongoing nationwide discussion and all parties agree that an overhaul of the system is needed. The Sláintecare strategy, described by the Irish government as a 'roadmap for building a world-class health and social care service', was meant to do just that. Its aim was to provide, through the appointment of an Oireachtas Committee, a cross-party vision on public health. The report, published in 2017, was welcomed by Sinn Féin as an opportunity 'to make history'. However, health spokesperson Louise Reilly lamented the following year the lack of progress on the matter (PR, 5/07/18). The party fully endorsed the plan in its 2020 manifesto, seeing it as a way to introduce a long-held vision – that of a universal, all-Ireland public health care system, 'free at the point of entry'.

Equally emblematic of Sinn Féin's identity is its flagship policy on housing. The issue had been making headlines in the Irish media for some time before the 2020 elections, as the country was experiencing a dire shortage of affordable housing, as well as high levels of homelessness. Construction was also at a low point and demand could not be met, leading to a hike in prices and hence in rents, pushing a high number of people out of the market. Analysts converge on the fact that government intervention is required in order to address the issue. Building new homes is one of the priorities, and while the number has increased (from less than 10,000 in 2016 to 21,000 in 2019), this is still deemed insufficient. Equally important is developing social housing. While the annual target set by the Minister for Housing is 7,736, only 10% of that target was reached in 2020 due to the COVID-19 crisis. The target itself was well below what Sinn Féin advocated in its manifesto, proposing a yearly construction of 20,000 public homes on average to meet needs.

Sinn Féin's main architect in terms of housing policy is Eoin Ó Broin. His book *Home* is the fruit of academic research which takes a holistic look at the housing policies of the Irish State since its foundation in 1921. His observations are quite stark. The housing crisis is a misnomer, as it is not a crisis, it is a failure of a 'dysfunctional' system. Housing has been viewed as a commodity, rather than a social necessity, which has resulted in the 'under-provision of public non-market housing and an over-reliance on the private market to meet housing needs' (Ó Broin, 2019, 11). This shortage of social housing has resulted in 'increasing reliance on the private rental sector to meet social housing needs' and led to an 'ever greater demand for rental properties, pushing up prices across the sector' (Ó Broin, 2019, 91). The COVID-19 crisis has further shrunk the buying market and pushed prices up further (up 3.5%).

One of the many consequences of the ongoing crisis is the increase in homelessness, which between July 2014 and October 2020 rose by 232% (Focus Ireland, 2020). The Department of Housing, Local Government and Heritage publishes monthly statistics, which put the total figure in October 2020 at 8,737 (6,095 adults and 2,642 dependants), with the 24–44-year-old age group disproportionately affected.[24] Interestingly, the COVID-19 crisis initially saw a decrease in the rate of homelessness, as in February 2020 the total number was 10,148. This, according to NGO Focus Ireland, shows that measures such as moratoriums on evictions and rent freezes,[25] both introduced during the pandemic, and both advocated by the not-for-profit sector, are efficient tools to combat homelessness. Sinn Féin's programme for addressing this issue included rent freezes and reducing the time spent in emergency accommodation.

Sinn Féin, along with other parties and homeless not-for-profit organisations, such as Focus Ireland or the Simon Community, advocates for the right to housing to be enshrined in the Irish constitution. Gerry Adams introduced a private member's bill to that effect in the Dáil in May 2016. The proposal was subsequently endorsed by parties such as Labour, People Before Profit and the Social Democrats, and an advocacy group, Home for Good, was formed to canvas on the holding of a referendum. Commenting on a 2019 report by the Oireachtas Library & Research Services which she had commissioned, Independent Senator Colette Kelleher stated that 'The current constitutional protections are being interpreted in restrictive and ambiguous ways. They are obstructive, and are contributing to the housing crisis. Housing is the single biggest domestic issue of our time, and we need radical and bold measures to address it' (Kelleher blog, 03/09/19). Part of Sinn Féin's approach is to shift the focus from emergency accommodation provision, which accounts for 95% of government spending in this area, to homelessness prevention. To this end, the party used its private member bill to propose a Homeless Prevention Bill in December 2020, aimed at 'Empowering and resourcing local authorities to assist families before they lose their home' (PR, 03/11/20).

Sinn Féin's commitment in the area of social justice and social policy had undoubtedly paid off, as reflected in the party's overall electoral performance. In Northern Ireland, it has steadily increased its share of the vote, overtaking its main rival, the SDLP, in the 2001 Assembly election and keeping its advance ever since. Obviously, Sinn Féin's performance at the polls is, like any other parties', heavily dependent on the context in which the election takes place. Therefore, in the 2019 Westminster election, it lost 6.7% of its vote, decreasing from 29.4% in 2017 to 22.8%. This drop can be ascribed to a number of factors, such as the fatigue of the electorate with the suspension of the authorities, which also impacted the performance of its main rival, the DUP, down 5.4% (BBC, 19/12/19). Sinn Fein experienced a similar electoral decline in the Republic in 2019 as it did in Northern

Ireland, both at EU and local levels, with the loss of 78 seats in the local elections (a drop of 4.4% of the vote) and the defeat of two of its three MEPs, in what were the first elections since McDonald had taken over from Adams as leader of the party. An internal review was undertaken to identify the issues that had cost the party its drop at the polls. Eoin Ó Broin explained that 'people want positive opposition, they want alternatives, they want things to be fixed, and I think if we can continue to argue in an ever increasing number of areas that we have credible policies that, if and when in government, we will implement, whether it's on childcare, pensions, public transport, climate, I think the party can grow' (Ó Broin, interview, August 2020). Sinn Féin's 2020 electoral success was the result of its efforts to strengthen its identity as a party with solid proposals on a number of issues, to counter the perception that it was merely a populist, protest party. Mary Lou McDonald analysed the manner in which they were able to regain the lost ground in the following manner: 'Politically, what we have concluded is that there was a bit of confusion amongst our electoral base. What I mean by that is when austerity was at its peak, and when people were under massive pressure and the cuts were really vicious, people understood and understand that you can turn to Sinn Féin to stand your ground, to stand up for you' (IE, 07/09/20). As one TD put it bluntly, 'We seemed unable to move past the anger into the recovery mode. Mary Lou had made her name taking Enda Kenny and others to the cleaners but she and we all realised a new approach was needed' (IE, 07/09/20). This approach, essentially, consisted in doing what Sinn Féin does best: being a grassroots party.

Visibility matters

While Sinn Féin's progress is due to its increased politicisation, its role in the peace process and the prioritisation of electoral policies, it is also, and perhaps more importantly, due to a well thought-out strategy that prioritises visibility. This means maintaining a constant presence in the political space that they see as having been left vacant by the depoliticisation of many. 'People have lost faith in politics, people don't actually believe that there can be political change', says Galway TD Mairéad Farrell (interview, September 2020), a view that is echoed by her colleague, Roscommon TD Claire Kerrane (interview, September 2020). Being there, physically and virtually, has been a long-held, two-pronged strategy at which the party excels: grounding its presence in the community, and ensuring that the message is constantly aired, either through traditional or social media.

Sinn Féin is a party of activists. This is enshrined in its constitution. 'All Sinn Féin members, whether cumann [local section] members or not, are expected to be activists'. When joining, members are committing to carrying out a number of activities, and an education course is 'mandatory for all applicants who wish to become cumann members'.[26] But Sinn Féin's grassroots strategy is not a recent development. In the early years of the Troubles, it was all the more important not to operate in a vacuum, as not only was the party banned in Northern Ireland – its main theatre of operation – until 1974, but it did not take part in electoral contests and thus had to find alternative ways of representing its supporters. This context is behind the strong grassroots approach to politics that has been retained to this day, albeit in different forms.

In January 1975, the Provisional IRA announced a ceasefire, after negotiations with representatives from the Catholic and Protestant Churches in December 1974 in Feakle (Co Clare). In order to monitor events on the grounds, the British authorities and the republican leadership agreed to open 'incident centres', which were to liaise between the two sides in case, according to Secretary of State Merlyn Rees, 'difficulties about the ceasefire arrangements emerge' (IT, 12/02/75). However, Sinn Féin soon realised the potential that such centres offered. Their objective was extended to include '[publicising] Sinn Féin, as a citizens' advice bureau, and as the nerve centre of all local Sinn Féin activity' (Craig, 2014, 317). By the time Sinn Féin entered its first electoral contest, in 1982, the centres had become fully operational political clinics, broadening their remit even further. 'Less than two years after, there were 28 such centres, open to the public every weekday, and dealing with issues such as housing, social security, local disputes or "harassment by security forces"' (IT, 18/01/84). Beyond the benefits generated in terms of local representation, this also meant that Sinn Féin personnel were acquiring first-hand knowledge and experience of the operation of

State institutions and policies. The centres also offered a platform to recruit new members and spread the message. But, more fundamentally, they fed into the party's narrative on the legitimacy of the State. Working with official bodies that dealt with housing, employment or public health was a necessary compromise, and Sinn Féin took on the role of mediator on behalf of the people it represented. It could thus offer an alternative to the institutions in place. A 1986 flyer presented the advice centres in the following way: 'Are you harassed, threatened, intimidated? Then contact Sinn Féin, for advice, help and support'. From this approach to politics emerged a new type of supporter, the 'organic intellectual', who, while not necessarily a member of the party, helped to 'articulate and reinforce the ideological values of republicanism on the local level and to provide organisational leadership. These efforts facilitate the work of the party both in rallying electoral support in these communities and also in transmitting issues of local concern to Sinn Féin leadership for policy consideration' (Cassidy, 2005, 343).

Currently, there are twenty-eight such offices in Northern Ireland (six for Belfast alone), and sixteen in the Republic. As the community is at the heart of the strategy, these centres act as a point of contact between the national and the local. Ó Snodaigh explains that his constituency office works in conjunction with the local representatives and the MEP for the area (until 2019 when she lost her seat). Their function is mainly to reflect what people are saying on the ground (from the 'hole in the road' to housing), but also, in some cases, to 'educate':

'You have to listen to the community and we have to mould our policies to reflect that, but there are policies that I hold on a principled stance. There was an argument against a traveller site during COVID-19 and some people objected to it, but I could not argue against [this site]' (Ó'Snodaigh, interview, August 2020).

Visibility and commitment are thus of the essence for a party that is constantly on the campaign trail, since it runs for election twice as often as most of its competitors as it puts up candidates on both sides of the border. Between the years 2015 and 2020, Sinn Féin took part in 12 different campaigns, at national and local levels: three Westminster general elections (2016, 2017, 2019); two Dáil elections (2016, 2020); local elections and European elections, fought on both sides of the border in 2019; one Assembly election (2017); and finally, three referenda: Marriage Equality (2015), Brexit (2016), Repeal the Eighth (2018). But maintaining a presence on the ground, while highly important, is only one part of this strategy. Its communication style and its engagement on social media give the party an edge over its competitors. Creating their own communication channels was always seen as a priority, in order to offer a counter-narrative to that of the mainstream media. This was all the more relevant during the Troubles, when censorship measures were introduced in both jurisdictions. In the Republic, Section 31 of the Broadcasting Act came into force in 1971 and forbade the broadcast of interviews with members of a number of organisations, including Sinn Féin. It took the UK seventeen more years to introduce a similar ban, which soon became redundant, as the media got around it by hiring actors to dub the interviewees' voices.[27]

But Sinn Féin's focus on communication predated the conflict. With every split or every major reorganisation came new publications. In 1948 it was *United Irishman*, in 1970, *An Phoblacht* (Dublin) and *Republican News* (Belfast), until these two weekly publications merged in 1979. The Director of Publicity is a high ranking post as the holder is a member of the restrained Ard Comhairle Office Board. Sinn Fein is the only party to produce its own weekly publication, *An Phoblacht*, one of the many outlets that ensure that an unfiltered message can be put across to its members and supporters. *An Phoblacht*, which original title dates back to 1907, was revamped in 1970 and became the Republican movement's banner for almost 50 years, until it decided to put an end to its print format and go fully online at the end of 2017, switching to a magazine edition which first issue was made available in March 2018.

Sinn Féin admits that social media particularly suits the party. As Director of Communication Ciarn Quinn explained, 'The traditional republican approach is using direct methods to talk directly to people. Don't get me wrong, we have pointy elbows when it comes to traditional media. In the past we bypassed that with murals and our own newspaper. Now it's social media' (*IT*, 02/02/16). Fine Gael's Neale Richmond admits that on that front, they are 'head and shoulders above anyone else' (Richmond, interview, April 2020). This was confirmed by the findings of a study of the political parties' presence on the internet during the 2020 elections, which assessed Sinn Féin's engagement on Facebook as 10 times that of the other political parties. As importantly, the interaction with Sinn Féin posts on Facebook was more than tenfold what it was for the other two parties: 567,020 as opposed to 49,358 for Fianna Fáil and 55,152 for Fine Gael (*IT*, 25/05/20).

Sinn Féin is, by far, the most active party on social media and the one who has the highest number of followers, across all four platforms, as Table 2 illustrates. Undoubtedly, Sinn Féin has a lot to gain by this online media exposure. According to a study published in the *Irish Times*, during the last week of the campaign, it spent less than its competitors on its online campaign, but used it better. Online memes therefore contributed to the shaping of opinions among the most social media savvy, the younger generation. Throughout the COVID-19 pandemic, Sinn Féin ensured a visible presence by using the YouTube channel to organise events, such as commemorations, announcements by Northern Ireland ministers, online discussions and debates. While the uptake from viewers is modest, ranging from 500 to the more common 3,000 views, it nevertheless constitutes a back catalogue of all Sinn Féin's activities and its public stances on varied topics, from the predictable Brexit explainer and COVID-19 updates and debate to statements on mental health and suicide or education. Interestingly, those videos that get most views (ranging from 30,000 to 40,000) are commemorations, such as Martin McGuinness on his 70th birthday (37,000

Table 2 *Sinn Féin's engagement with social media, 2020*

| | Facebook | Twitter | | Instagram | | YouTube | |
	Followers	Followers	Tweets	Followers	Posts	Subscribers	Views
Sinn Féin	265,761	147.9K	62.2K	51.4K	1,411	31.2K	16,105,551
Fianna Fáil	42,690	49K	36K	7,309	1,355	1.78K	2,197,842
Fine Gael	43,372	25.1K	53.4	8,306	867	n/a	1,565,035

Source: data gathered by author on social media, 10/06/21.

views, 23/05/20) or of course Bobby Storey (92,000 views, 26/05/20).[28]

Nevertheless, the party's social media engagement can also backfire. A number of controversies have erupted, mainly due to tweets issued on public representatives' accounts. Barry McElduff's tweet about Kingsmill on the anniversary of the killing by the IRA of ten Protestants led to his resignation from his Westminster seat and from the party. In November 2020, Laois-Offaly TD Brian Stanley was embroiled in a double controversy. One concerned a tweet on the Warrenpoint attack in which the IRA killed 18 British soldiers in 1979, the other a 2017 tweet that was considered homophobic, which led to calls for his resignation as chair of the Oireachtas Committee on Finance. At the behest of the party leader he stepped out of politics for one week and also deleted his social media accounts. Kildare North TD Reada Cronin's blunt anti-Semitic comments generated a furore, and was one more issue that the leadership had to attend to by apologising unreservedly, although Party Finance spokesperson Pearse Doherty commented that some of those tweets had been posted before she had joined Sinn Féin (*BT*, 20/02/20). Obviously Sinn Féin representatives are not unique in posting offensive tweets. Fianna Fáil Senator Lorraine Clifford-Lee had to apologise in 2019 for past tweets that used derogatory language towards the Traveller community (*The Journal*, 12/11/19). The fact that these tweets are also the object of public controversies shows that Sinn Féin is not treated differently to its colleagues. However, there is no doubt that the role it seeks to play in the politics of the Irish Republic has led to a heightened level of scrutiny. But, as an editorial in the *Irish Times* put it, 'This is not, as some in the party's army of vocal online supporters have it, an establishment conspiracy to damage Sinn Féin. It is part of the normal and healthy process of politics and public debate in a democracy' (*IT*, 07/03/20). Weathering those storms and sustaining its credibility is one of the main challenges faced by the party.

Sinn Féin in government?

By winning most first preference votes in the 2020 general election, and securing 37 seats, Sinn Féin was not only tagging just behind Fianna Fáil's 38 seats, but was ahead of Fine Gael by 2 seats. This outcome was particularly spectacular given that Sinn Féin had fielded half the number of candidates (42) compared to its main competitors. The result generated momentous shifts within the political landscape. It challenged the bi-partisan status quo that had dominated Irish political life since the foundation of the State, which had guaranteed Fianna Fáil and Fine Gael a place in governments on a rotating basis. After protracted negotiations, certainly slowed down by the emergence of the COVID-19 pandemic, a historical alliance between Fine Gael and Fianna Fáil was formed in May 2020.

The results propelled Sinn Féin to a different level. Former Fine Gael trustee Mark Fitzgerald's analysis encapsulated what he saw as a double-edged outcome:

'Sinn Féin, leaving its earlier anti-European stance behind and choosing a left-wing Nationalism, rather than the right-wing xenophobia of Nationalist politics elsewhere, has contributed to our political culture. It has further allowed the party to capitalise on the frustrations of our younger generation, and has resulted in a wake-up call to the more orthodox political establishment'. But suspicion levels remained high: 'can Sinn Féin become more accountable, less attritional and stop pitting sections of society against each other?' asked the writer in the same article (*IT*, 19/10/20).

The fact that the party who had disrupted this status quo was Sinn Féin raised unprecedented questions for Irish political leaders. Until 2020, its progress could still be ascribed to a protest vote and while the Sinn Féin leaders themselves had been calling to be included in government in 2016, the likelihood of this scenario was somehow downplayed. A telling sign was the decision during the campaign by RTÉ to initially exclude Mary Lou McDonald from the final televised debate between the leaders of the two main parties. Under pressure, not only from Sinn Féin itself but also from public opinion as polls were clearly indicating what RTÉ referred to as the 'notable change in the dynamic of the campaign on the ground' (*IT*, 03/02/20), the national broadcaster reversed its decision. Mary Lou McDonald commented that 'the idea of having the two men who were in Government together for the last five years debating each other on their shared record is farcical' (*IT*, 03/02/20). The underlying message was that the days were over when women, and more to the point, Republican women, were absent from the highest political spheres.

The 2020 general election also revealed the breadth and scope of the inroads that Republicans had made in many different demographic categories, an outcome which might have surprised Sinn Féin itself. Age was one of the factors that was most commented upon, as a sizeable percentage of the 18–24 group gave Sinn Féin their first preference vote. Some of the newspaper headlines automatically assumed that this connection was not only evident but somehow, a new development: 'Youth Vote Sweeps Sinn Féin to Election Breakthrough' (*Hotpress*), 'Can Sinn Féin's young voters finally pull Ireland to the left?' (*Guardian*), 'How gen z helped Sinn Féin and the left triumph in Ireland's general election' (*Vice*). The increase in the vote was, however, substantial in all age categories, as shown in Table 3. Moreover, among the 6% who voted in 2020 but not in 2016, 45% were in the youngest age group (6%). While this does not necessarily indicate that this cohort voted for Sinn Féin, a possible correlation can be made between these two dimensions.

Table 3   *Increase in Sinn Féin's first preference vote, 2016–2020 (%)*

	Age group				
	18–24	25–34	35–49	50–64	65+
2016	22.4	25.1	16.1	13.9	9.9
2020	31.8	31.7	22	22.8	12.2

Source: Ipsos MRBI Exit Poll, *Irish Times*, 08/02/20 and 09/02/20.

The *Irish Times* was more moderate in its appraisal of the Sinn Fein youth vote. 'Election not a "youthquake" but desire for change across electorate' was how Kieran O'Leary qualified the outcome (*IT*, 19/02/20). The results indicated, in his view, a political shift from the previous generation, one where the IRA was not only in a distant past but somehow rendered redundant. This was ascribed to the fact that the younger generation hadn't lived through the Troubles, implying that they could not connect in the same manner with the atrocities as their parent's generation as they did not have the lived experiences of these events. While this analysis is undoubtedly pertinent, it tends to focus on the capacity of the younger generation to turn the page, to leave the past in the past. The posting of IRA memes on social media, and particularly on TikTok, has been seen as a potential glorification of terrorism. Undoubtedly disturbing for those who have gone through the bleakest times of the conflict, the 'memefication of the IRA' is a complex phenomenon which includes irony and irreverence, and that can be seen as revealing 'inevitably shifting norms' while 'helping normalise a language and a culture that still has the power to shock a demographic old enough to remember when it was used without irony' (*IT*, 15/02/20).

Besides, linking the youth vote with a disconnect from Sinn Féin's history tends to strip the vote of its ideological dimension, at least in part. A hypothetical severance of the party with its past would not make it more attractive to those who disagree with their socio-economic views. Moreover, the exit polls highlighted a number of points of convergence between the younger elector-ate and Sinn Féin, with 75% in favour of holding a poll between the North and the South within five years and 68% believing that Fianna Fáil and Fine Gael were wrong to rule out the formation of a government with Sinn Féin. The exit poll revealed other interesting indicators that gave some insight into the profile of the average Sinn Féin voters. Only half of them had decided how they would vote before the start of the campaign. This is good news for the party, insofar as it shows that it has made inroads far beyond its own base and that it is capable of staging a strong and convincing campaign. Claire Kerrane, while canvassing in a rural, and older, constituency, that of Roscommon, also found that the themes developed by her party 'got a lot of interest on the doorsteps' (Kerrane, interview, 10/20). Nevertheless, this finding could also be of concern for the party, as it could indicate that its electorate is still somewhat volatile. Ó Broin is aware of the need to keep that constituency on board:

> those gains can slip away from us as quickly as they came and we are very conscious of that. I think there are two or three things we need to do, the first is to remain true to our policy objectives that convinced those people to vote for us in the first place, so if an increasing number of younger people voted for us because of our policies on housing, we need to keep advocating those policies but crucially we need to get into government to implement those policies. (Ó Broin, interview, August 2020)

Keeping housing at the top of its agenda is one way in which the party remains in touch with this electorate, who still rates health and housing as the two most pressing issues, as demonstrated with Ó Broin's introduction of the Homeless Prevention Bill in the Dáil in November 2020 but also by the many tweets and videos posted on Facebook on the issue.

Sinn Féin was adamant that the results clearly signalled the people's desire for its representatives to be included in any future government, and multiplied statements to that effect in the aftermath of the election. However, such calls might have been destined mainly for internal ears. Indeed, relying on numbers solely to make this claim was a logical but somewhat weak argument. Forming part of a coalition government was not on the cards for 2020, as both Fianna Fáil and Fine Gael had ruled out this option, in no uncertain terms, in the run-up to polling day. The strong performance of Sinn Féin candidates changed the story, but not enough for Fianna Fáil, in particular, to make a U-turn. For some Republican supporters, this pointed to a contradiction, as the same parties that exclude Sinn Féin from any government prospect in the Republic had been arguing for the institutions in the North to be restored and for a power-sharing Executive to be formed. Thus Sinn Féin's presence in the Northern Ireland Executive is strongly encouraged. While parties in the Republic have the choice of deciding not to share power with Sinn Féin, this is not something that is afforded to their political opponents in Northern Ireland. Fine Gael TD Neale Richmond does not see this as a contradiction. 'We're in this position because we have moved on. Northern Ireland is still in a post conflict situation' (Richmond, interview, April 2020).

Indeed, there are a number of reasons for the two main parties' reluctance to go into government with Sinn Féin. One is, bluntly, their differing worldviews. As Richmond observes, 'we disagree on practically everything' (interview, April 2020), which could also be said of Sinn Féin and the DUP, as their major divergences are not solely on constitutional issues. Another is lack of trust. In order to be in any governing coalition, Sinn Féin still has to convince its potential partners that it has definitely put its past behind. This means, for Fine Gael Minister Patrick O'Donovan, clearly stating that they recognise all institutions as legitimate, including 'only one army in this country – Óglaigh na hÉireann – the Irish Defence Forces and the Special Criminal Court' (PR, 25/02/20). This last point can be partly traced to a proposal in previous Sinn Féin manifestos that the Special Criminal Court and the Special Powers Act, both introduced in 1939 when the IRA had embarked on a short-lived campaign in England, be abolished, as they were 'relics of the Troubles'. The debate on the Special Criminal Court emerged after the signing of the GFA. The Hederman report on the review of the emergency legislation fell short of recommending its abolition, although the minority opinion called for the Special Criminal court to be 'dispensed with' (par 9.96). However, the party recently changed its position and McDonald stated during the leaders' debate of the 2020 campaign that 'I accept that we need mechanisms and special powers. What we have been calling for the last four years is for a review led by a High Court judge to ensure that the courts, the Gardaí the DPP's office have the full resources that they need to keep people safe' (*IT*, 05/02/20).

Another criticism levied at Sinn Féin is its lack of transparency and its centralised operation. The party constitution sets out the different levels of operation and their functions, and mentions the 'Coiste Seasta', a group of eight members who have full power to carry out routine business between Ard Chomhairle meetings. An *Irish Times* article noted that 'It had only one elected representative and three of its members had IRA convictions' (*IT*, 05/03/20). However, this is not necessarily problematic in the eyes of a party within which prisoners have played a key role. Furthermore, as Sinn Fein Director of Finance Des Mackin commented, 'We don't want a parliamentary party running the organisation. We want to stay a party of activists. It's a totally different model. There's nothing mysterious about it' (*IT*, 05/03/20).

Sinn Féin is also frequently categorised as a populist party, a term which has acquired negative connotations in recent times. Varadkar tweeted on 13 February 2020: 'More evidence that Sinn Fein is Ireland's populist party. They don't believe in science – whether it's vaccines or the need for a carbon tax'.[29] Micheál Martin, while not branding Sinn Féin as populist, affirmed that it had consistently 'been fomenting an anti-EU approach and they take stances within EU parliament which is concerning in my view' (*IT*, 02/05/19). *Irish Examiner* columnist Michael Clifford stated in the aftermath of the elections that 'populism has arrived here, albeit a very Irish populism' (*IE*, 01/02/20). Undoubtedly, there is a strong identification between Sinn Féin and the people, which is a frequently used term both in its public discourse and in its policy documents, as well as a tendency to make binary class oppositions, and a strong social media engagement, all considered trademarks of populism. In the context of the debate on the rise of populism after the 2008 crisis, the term has gained traction and is generally connected to expressions of extreme political views. But Sinn Féin doesn't share the extreme Euroscepticism of most of its European counterparts. Its position is one of 'critical engagement with the EU', meaning that while it remains critical of the general socio-economic orientation of the supranational organisation it engages with its institutions. The Nationalist background of Sinn Féin is also used as a shortcut to align the party with populist Nationalist parties, but this is unfounded given the pro-immigration stances that Sinn Féin has taken since the start of the century. Sinn Féin Chairman Declan Kearney considered this labelling a lazy attempt to 'dismiss' their electoral success (*AP*, 21/12/16). Moreover, this categorisation is not something that everyone in Sinn Féin is uncomfortable with. Ó Broin explains that 'Populism is a strategy, to advance a political project. It can be deployed by left or right wing parties. I define Sinn Féin as a left republican party. There are elements in our strategy that are populist, absolutely, just as Sanders or Corbyn. I do think, however, that there is a challenge for democratic left-wing parties who occupy that populist space, they have yet to define circumstances of governing and of taking power' (Ó Broin, interview, August 2020).

Conclusion

In 2021, Northern Ireland celebrated its centenary: one hundred years of partition, fifty of which were spent under the rule of the Unionist-dominated Stormont regime, thirty under violent conflict, and twenty under the newfound, if fragile, peace that all, or almost all, cherish and value. Yet this celebration is a stark reminder that the fault-lines over the legacy of the Troubles and the existence of partition itself are still deep. Moreover, this anniversary coincided with the British departure from the EU, in what Unionists hope will reinforce Northern Ireland's status within the UK, while Nationalists see a potential for increased North–South cooperation. Such celebrations will heighten the binary feelings of belonging between those who view Northern Ireland within the UK as their pride and joy and those who still feel that there is unfinished business. Neither the SDLP nor Sinn Féin accepted the invitation to take part in the Northern Ireland Centenary Forum, established in September 2019 to organise the events. But the manner in which both

Unionists and Nationalists expressed their positioning on the constitutional status of Northern Ireland was not antagonistic, showing how far society has come since the GFA. Sinn Féin Finance Minister Conor Murphy explained his party's position in the following manner: 'There will be celebrations for some people; for other people it is a period of reflection to look at the impact that partition has had on this island for 100 years and all the negative consequences that have flowed from that'. This conciliatory tone was matched by that of the UUP: 'Inevitably, there will be those who take a different view, and in a free society they are quite entitled to do so, but that will not detract from those of us who are proud to call this place home'. The British Secretary of State confidently concluded that 'The way people have come together across communities to support each other through Covid bodes well for the future' (*BT*, 15/12/20). However, the fact that this future is still so rooted in the past shows how divided Northern Ireland remains.

The year 2021 was the anniversary of the signing of the Treaty that officially brought into existence two autonomous States on the island of Ireland. It also paved the way for the fratricide civil war, which outcome divided the Free State for generations to come and which wounds are still not fully closed, as seen with the controversy over the RIC. Sinn Féin will not have much to celebrate on either side of the border, as both anniversaries mark events that Republicans staunchly opposed. But the party sees the prospect of a United Ireland as closer than any time in the past hundred years, and displays an optimism for the future that might only really have been matched in the early years of the Northern Ireland conflict when the Provisionals were convinced of their own imminent victory. Sinn Féin is now a very different political organisation to what it has been at any time in its history. Its confidence in its own place within the Irish political landscape is undeniable. Roscommon TD Claire Kerrane embodies her party's enthusiasm and determination, certain of the inevitability of a United Ireland but one that will require a lot of hard work, something she is prepared to commit to, as shown in her persistent engagement in the electoral contest (Kerrane, interview, 10/20). Much like her colleagues in the North, such as Linda Dillon, she is convinced that she can work well within the present political climate and doesn't make much of the various controversies in which her party is embroiled from time to time. 'These kinds of conversations serve nobody. I don't want to add to the grief on both sides', she answered when asked by radio host Pat Kenny about the Brian Hanley tweets over the civil war in December 2020, thus 'kicking to touch with a proficiency that would shame an older generation' according to *Irish Times* radio commentator Mick Heaney (*IT*, 11/12/20).

The test that Sinn Féin, as any other party, needs to successfully and continuously pass, is that of elections. Fifteen months after its unexpected performance in the 2020 general election, the party still maintained a high approval rate, and had even succeeded in increasing its ratings with an average of 28–29% voting intentions between May 2020 and June 2021 (from 24% in the actual elections in February). This placed Sinn Féin ahead of its two main rivals, Fine Gael (at 28%) and Fianna Fáil (at 16%).[1] The themes that Sinn Fein has been championing, health and housing, are still also the top priorities of voters who feel that the government should increase spending in these areas. But this conversation is not exclusive to Sinn Féin and the party needs to find a way to keep its policies relevant and its voice distinct to that of others. Nine months after the general election, the party maintained a marked lead among the younger electorate, with 40% first preference votes among the 18–24 age group as opposed to 25% for Fine Gael and 10% for Fianna Fáil (*IT*, 07/10/20). It is this constituency that the party must hold on to, not only in terms of its future political progress, but also because the new generation no longer ascribes to a Sinn Fein vote the value that their parents might have, and no longer really cares to make the connection with the IRA a priority. Retaining this stronghold will strengthen its hand when it comes to claiming its place in a future coalition government. One hundred years after the creation of the Free State which Sinn Féin so vehemently opposed, the party is prepared, and willing, to reshape Irish politics for the decades to come.

Notes

Chapter 1

1 Until 1933, all members of Dáil Éireann not only swore allegiance to the constitution of the Free State but also recognised
   the British monarch as the head of the 'associated states'.
2 Founded in 1931, this radical left-wing organisation faced
   staunch opposition from conservative forces, amongst whom
   the Catholic Church, who strongly advised its followers not to
   join. It was banned in 1931 as part of a 'red scare' campaign.
3 Founded in 1934 by a splinter group from the IRA who had
   refused to back it up as a successor to Saor Éire.
4 In 1932, the IRA supported Fianna Fáil, albeit reluctantly on
   some issues, in the general election, which strained the relationships between the two organisations. Attempts were made
   at working out compromises, but Sinn Féin was once again
   discarded as a potential political wing when the IRA founded
   Cumann Poblachta na hÉireann in 1936 to contest by-elections.
5 In Republican history, the Second Dáil, elected in 1921 before
   the signing of the Treaty, was the last legitimate Assembly.
   Those of its members who rejected the Treaty and the Free
   State constituted a small circle of deputies from the pre-civil
   war era who retained the name 'Second Dáil', They were seen
   for decades as the guardians of republican orthodoxy, and while
   their numbers dwindled, they were still called upon when
   momentous decisions were taken by the organisation. Thus, on

the eve of the split in 1970, future Provisional Sinn Féin leaders Ruairí Ó Bradáigh and Daithí Ó Conaill sought and obtained the support of the only surviving Second Dáil member Tom Maguire.

6 This 1934 statement has often been misquoted as 'a Protestant parliament for a Protestant people', when he was in fact refer-ring to the Free State, which according to him 'boasted of being a Catholic State'. He did, however, later state that his duty was to ensure that employees of the State would be loyal to the King and constitution, as in his view, 'this is my whole object in carrying on a protestant government for a protestant people'. See https://cain.ulster.ac.uk/issues/discrimination/quotes.htm.

7 Following the electoral success of Bobby Sands and other pris-oners on hunger strike in the Westminster and Dáil elections in 1981, Sinn Féin opted for a strategy that would combine mil-itary and political approaches, in view of maintaining pressure on the British and Irish political leaders and to obtain an elec-toral mandate. This strategy took its name from a statement made by then Director of Publicity Danny Morrison at his party's Ard Fheis in 1981: 'Who here really believes we can win the war through the ballot box? But will anyone here object if, with a ballot paper in this hand and an Armalite in the other, we take power in Ireland?' (Hannigan, 1985).

8 Poll of British electorate: 23% in favour of union with Republic, 31% independent state, 29% remain part of UK, 17% no opin-ion (IT, 25/03/1992).

9 For a more detailed analysis of Sinn Féin's electoral progress, see chapter 3.

10 'The Irish people need to reclaim the spirit of 1916, which is not the property of those who have abused and debased the title of republicanism' (IT, 22/10/05).

11 While Fianna Fáil presented itself in 2007 as having 'led the debate on unity', the issue was entirely absent from its 2011 programme, and only mentioned once in 2016. In the 2020 manifesto, Fianna Fáil held that 'unity within a shared state would be to the social, economic and cultural benefit of all the people of our island' but put the focus on consensus. Fine Gael, for its part, is less committed to the unity of the island, which

was only mentioned in its 2016 manifesto in a cautionary manner, welcoming the increased North–South cooperation.

12 See chapter 3.

13 Teachta Dála: Member of the Dáil Éireann, the Irish parliament.

14 https://aontu.ie/.

15 The expression was used by Mary Lou McDonald on 31 January 2020 when meeting with members of the Border Communities Against Brexit group, created in the aftermath of the referendum to protect the interests of those most affected by Brexit along the border (McDonald, YouTube, 31/01/20).

16 J. Garry (2016–2017) 'The EU referendum vote in Northern Ireland: implications for our understanding of citizens' political views and behaviour', www.qub.ac.uk/brexit/Brexitfilestore/Filetoupload,728121,en.pdf.

17 'Uniting Ireland – a Sinn Féin public discussion', www.youtube.com/watch?v=tiXQMFiKYg8.

18 An investigation was launched to examine whether the amounts gained by applicants to the scheme amounted to corruption or were due to mismanagement and incompetence. Its report was published on 20 March 2020 and concluded, among other things, that the selection and role of special advisers should be overhauled.

19 The logjam was broken in January 2020 with the *New Decade, New Approach* agreement that paved the way for the restoration of the power-sharing Executive, which provided, inter alia, for the official recognition of both Irish and Ulster-Scots.

20 The document, *Securing Designated Special Status for the North within the EU*, made a series of concrete proposals, such as continued representation of Northern Ireland within the EU, and called for any agreement on the status of Northern Ireland to be agreed by both Irish and British governments.

21 Of the other four issues, only climate change has led to a concrete outcome, with the setting up of a parliamentary commission to assess the report.

22 This was the third letter sent to Varadkar by this group, after a first one in 2017 gathered over 200 signatures and a second one more than 1,000 signatures in December 2018. The group adopts a similar line to that of Sinn Féin on Brexit, which it interprets as 'English nationalism [having] imposed an economic border

in the Irish Sea. Irish nationalism didn't. English nationalism has delivered an economic united Ireland and will impose it' (*IT*, 10/09/20).

23 The term pan-nationalist was first used to describe the loose and informal coalition between the Irish government and nationalist parties throughout the peace process. Some Unionists saw the calls for a United Ireland as the resurgence of pan-nationalism which made a false connection between the weakening of the union and Brexit, as in their view, 'to vote Remain was not to vote for a united Ireland in the event of Brexit' (*IT*, 19/03/18).

24 The nVivo software was used to perform the linguistic analysis.

25 This is a web page on the Sinn Féin website dedicated exclusively to reunification. It contains resources such as opinion polls, articles from various newspapers, reports and Sinn Féin party policy programmes, as well as a table listing all the interventions since 2018 in favour of a United Ireland, from different political and social perspectives, www.sinnfein.ie/irish-unity.

26 This is also the age group that votes most for Sinn Féin, see chapter 3.

27 In 1987, Sinn Féin sought to establish a wide nationalist movement which would include Sinn Féin, the SDLP, the Irish government and Irish America as a 'viable alternative to armed struggle' (O'Donnell, 2007, 231).

28 An Anti-Partition League was formed in 1945 in Northern Ireland and sought to enlist the support of political parties south of the border. However, it soon floundered as the political reality of the time did not make partition 'an issue at the top of the agenda in Dublin, London and Washington' (Lyn, 2005, 332).

Chapter 2

1 This initiative looks to commemorate the centenary of events from the period 1912 to 1922, starting with the Ulster covenant and ending with the civil war and the partition of Ireland. See www.decadeofcentenaries.com.

2 The ambush, during which two members of the RIC were killed, was not an operation sanctioned by the General Headquarters of

the Irish volunteers, but is regarded as the starting point of the War of Independence. See Flynn (1997).

3 Second official inquiry into the events of Bloody Sunday when fourteen civilians were shot dead by the British Army during a civil rights demonstration on 30 January 1972. The first enquiry, chaired by Lord Widgery, had largely absolved the soldiers. The Saville Enquiry, set up by Tony Blair's government in 1998, published its findings in 2010 and led to a public apology by the then Prime Minister David Cameron. Throughout the proceedings, many witnesses were called upon to testify, including Martin McGuinness, who made a statement in 2000.

4 From November 1982, women in the Armagh prison were frequently subjected to intrusive and arbitrary strip searches, which in the prison context have been considered a type of sexual abuse. See Wahidin & Powell (2017).

5 The IRA admitted to thirteen of those disappearances, the other three not being attributed to a specific organisation. By 2020, twelve bodies had been recovered by the Independent Commission for the Location of Victims Remains, which was set up in 1993 by the British and Irish governments. See www.iclvr.ie.

6 'Our day will come', rallying cry of the IRA, made all the more symbolic as it is the last line of Bobby Sands' auto-fictional account of his experience in the H-Blocks, *One Day in My Life* (Cork: Mercier Press, 1983).

7 Refers to the IRA which was active during the War of Independence.

8 Podcast available at: https://foreignaffairs.podbean.com/e/rich ard-haass-on-northern-ireland/.

9 Pat Finucane was killed in February 1989 by the Ulster Defence Association. However, it soon transpired that the assassination had been the outcome of collusion between the Loyalist paramilitaries and the British security services. This has been confirmed by two public investigations as well as a review. Therefore, relatives of the victim, as well as international organisations such as Amnesty International and the US House of Representatives, have been pressing for an independent, public inquiry. On 20 November 2020, the British government announced that 'now was not the time' for holding such an inquiry.

Chapter 3

1 See, for instance, 'Inside Business' with Ciarán Hancock, *Irish Times* weekly podcast.
2 See chapter 1 on Irish unity.
3 Owen Carron was Sands' electoral agent. He subsequently took the Westminster seat that Sands left vacant after his death.
4 In 1981, a number of candidates had been put forward by the National H-Blocks committee, mainly on the issue of the ongoing hunger strikes, and two had been elected. However, they were not Sinn Féin candidates as such. Therefore, the 1982 general election represented the first attempt by the party to run candidates in the Republic since 1957.
5 Caoimhghin Ó Caolain was the first ever Sinn Féin representative to take his seat in the Dáil. Elected in the Monaghan constituency, he was described at the time as representing 'a strain of traditional republicanism' (*IT*, 09/06/97).
6 Just like Sinn Féin, People Before Profit is an all-Ireland party. It contested the 2011 general election under the banner of the United Left Alliance with other radical parties and independent candidates.
7 235 local anti-water charges groups could be identified online: 67 were organised at the county level while 168 groups organised at the level of towns. 'Burn the bills' protests were held across at least 19 Irish counties. Local communities in at least 13 counties also held 'Bin the bills' events. Activists removing water meters at householders' requests, naming themselves 'Anti-water meter fairies', operated throughout most of the country.
8 Sinn Féin led the first preference votes with 7,288 compared with 6,540 for Murphy, but was defeated on the eighth count by a margin of 566 votes.
9 Yvonne Murphy (2016) describes the Marriage Equality referendum as one that 'clearly marked the transition of Irish society from one of the most socially conservative in Western Europe to a leader in the field of Lesbian, Gay, Bisexual and Transgender (LGBT) rights'.
10 www.sinnfein.ie/files/2009/Policies_LGB.pdf.

11 Sinn Féin published two different manifestos for the 2007 general election, one for its more general policies and one specifically for women.

12 The Eighth Amendment was introduced in 1983 to protect equally the rights of the mother and of the unborn child. This considerably restricted the possibility to legislate on abortion rights.

13 For a policy to become the official stance of the party, it needs to be approved at the annual Ard Fheis (Party Conference). The 1985 vote was thus reversed the following year and the policy was watered down to express empathy, ascribing termination of pregnancy solely to social and financial issues and no longer acknowledging the right to choose.

14 Online public debate organised by Neale Richmond, called 'A Shared island'.

15 This refers to the system of government put in place under the GFA, used in multi-ethnic or cultural states, which is predicated on the sharing of power by different sections of the community. Coalitions are thus embedded in the Northern Ireland institutions.

16 There were five failed attempts to introduce legislation in Stormont to provide for same-sex marriage between 2012 and 2015.

17 This is in line with the recommendations of the Report of the Inquiry concerning the United Kingdom of Great Britain and Northern Ireland under article 8 of the Optional Protocol to the Convention on the Elimination of All Forms of Discrimination against Women. Interestingly, it also included a provision to act on the payment to victims, www.legislation.gov.uk/ukpga/2019/22/contents/enacted.

18 @MaryLouMcdonald, 02/06/20, https://twitter.com/maryloumcdonald/status/1267796375300907009?lang=en.

19 Direct provision was introduced in 2000 by the Irish state to accommodate newly arrived asylum seekers. The system, the management of which was mainly outsourced to the private sector, and which was meant to provide for all basic needs, was criticised from the outset for a number of reasons: lack of basic amenities, overcrowding, deprivation of liberty, lack of autonomy, institutionalisation of its occupants, and isolation from

the community. Many NGOs and some political parties have been campaigning for its abolition on human rights grounds, and a number of reports have highlighted its inadequacies. The Fianna Fáil–Fine Gael coalition government has pledged to replace it by a not-for-profit system within its lifetime.

20 Ireland was, until recently, one of the only EU countries not to have hate crime legislation. In October 2019, the Department of Justice launched a consultation process to hear the general public's views on hate crime and hate speech. The Fianna Fáil/Fine Gael programme for government included the introduction of such legislation as part of their commitment. The Hate Crime Bill, which had originally been introduced as a private member's bill in 2017, was in Seanad Éireann as of December 2020.

21 The expression 'these Irish children' refers here to children born in Ireland whose parents are not Irish or EU nationals.

22 This poll was conducted in the context of the case of Eric Zhi Ying Xue, a young boy born in Ireland of a Chinese mother who was facing deportation.

23 Sinn Féin was, for instance, among the first parties to openly advocate for the end of direct provision and the introduction of the right to work for asylum seekers (Maillot, 2019).

24 Sinn Féin's Eoin Ó Broin puts the real figure at 10,522, as the official figure does not take into account those living in emergency accommodation, those living in domestic violence refuges, asylum seekers who have been granted the right to remain but are trapped in direct provision, or people sleeping rough.

25 Focus Ireland also included among the reasons for the decrease in homelessness the changes in behaviour caused by the pandemic, rather than the eviction embargo – for instance, people who were at risk of homelessness seeking alternative short-term options such as moving in with extended family or remaining in overcrowded or unsuitable accommodation, in preference to entering hostels during lockdown.

26 These activities include 'Electoral work; Community, Trade Union or other suitable external activism that benefits the party; Publicity Work (internet, etc.) on behalf of the party; Raising Finance Policy Formulation; Recruiting; *An Phoblacht* sales;

Attending Political Events & Commemorations; Participation in or Running of a network; [republican support networks or sectoral based networks, e.g. trade union networks, education networks, etc.]; All other activities that promote Sinn Féin aims and objectives'. Membership Rules and Regulations, Sinn Féin, 2016/17, www.derrysinnfein.ie/wp-content/uploads/2018/02/ sf_partydev_membershiprules.pdf.

27 Both bans were lifted in 1994.

28 Page accessed on 20/04/21.

29 @leo.varadkar, 13/02/20, https://twitter.com/leovaradkar/stat us/1227918074273304576?lang=en. This came when the content of a tweet by former Sinn Féin MEP Liadh Ní Riada was revealed, saying she would not give her daughter the HPV vaccine. She later stated she was not 'anti vax', and Sinn Féin explained that this did not 'reflect Sinn Féin policy' (*IT*, 16/02/20).

Conclusion

1 www.politico.eu/europe-poll-of-polls/ireland/.

Bibliography

All online sources were live as of 20 May 2021.

Primary sources

Interviews

Aiken, Steve, Ulster Unionist Party, MLA for East Antrim, April 2020.
Archibald, Caoimhe, MLA for East Derry, October 2020.
Campbell, Gregory, Democratic Unionist Party, August 2020.
Dillon, Linda, Sinn Féin, MLA for Mid Ulster, September 2020.
Farrell, Mairéad, TD for Galway West, September 2020.
Kerrane, Claire, Sinn Féin, TD for Roscommon, September 2020.
Ó Broin, Eoin, TD for Dublin Mid-West, Spokesperson on Housing, August 2020.
Ó Snodaigh, Aengus, TD for Dublin South-Central, August 2020.
Richmond, Neale, Fine Gael, TD for Dublin Rathdown, April 2020.

Newspapers and news outlets

AP   *An Phoblacht*
BT   *Belfast Telegraph*

DD   *Dáil Debates*
IE   *Irish Examiner*
II   *Irish Independent*
IT   *Irish Times*
LSE   London School of Economics
PR   Press Release
RTÉ   Raidió Teilifís Éireann (Irish public broadcaster)

Reports, blogs and websites

Adams, Gerry (YouTube, 10/04/18), 'Good Friday Agreement a Journey Not a Destination', www.youtube.com/watch?v=2iU7 yggx7Ig.

Bloomfield, Kenneth (1998), *We Will Remember Them, Report of the Northern Ireland Victims Commissioner*, Stationary Office, Northern Ireland, https://cain.ulster.ac.uk/issues/victims/docs/bloomfield98.pdf.

CAIN Archive, 'Conflict and Politics in Northern Ireland', https://cain.ulster.ac.uk/.

CGP (Consultative Group on the Past) (2009), *Report*, 23 January, https://cain.ulster.ac.uk/victims/docs/consultative_group/cgp_230109_report.pdf.

Daly, Mark (2017), *Brexit and the Future of Ireland: Uniting Ireland & its People in Peace & Prosperity*, Houses of the Oireachtas, Joint Committee on the Implementation of the Good Friday Agreement, https://webarchive.oireachtas.ie/parliament/media/committees/implementationofthego odfridayagreement/jcigfa2016/brexit-and-the-future-of-irel and.pdf.

—— (2019), *Unionist Concerns and Fears of a United Ireland: The Need to Protect the Peace Process and Build a Vision for a Shared Island and a United People*, Joint Oireachtas Committee on the Implementation of the Good Friday Agreement, https://senatormarkdaly.files.wordpress.com/2019/07/unionist-report.pdf.

Department of Foreign Affairs, www.dfa.ie/our-role-policies/no rthern-ireland/the-good-friday-agreement-and-today/ (includes links to most agreements since 1998).

Doherty, Pearse (YouTube, 05/07/20), 'Uniting Ireland – a Sinn Féin Online Public Discussion', www.youtube.com/watch?v=tiXQ MFiKYg8.

DUP (2019), 'Let's Get the UK Moving Again', *2019 General Election Manifesto*, www.politico.eu/wp-content/uploads/2019/11/024 156-DUP-Party-Manifesto.pdf.

Ending the Harm, www.endingtheharm.com.

European Commission, *State of Health in the EU, Ireland Country Health Report 2019*, https://ec.europa.eu/health/sites/health/files/state/docs/2019_chp_ir_english.pdf.

EU website on integration (04/02/20) *Irish General Election 2020 – What do Parties Say About Immigration and Integration?*, https://ec.europa.eu/migrant-integration/.

Fanning, Bryan, Jo Shaw, Jane-Ann O'Connell and Marie Williams (2007) 'Irish Political Parties, Immigration and Integration in 2007', UCD, www.ucd.ie/mcri/report.pdf.

Fine Gael (2014) *Constitution*, www.finegael.ie/app/uploads/2017/05/FG-Constitution-2014-Aug.pdf.

Focus Ireland (2020), *About Homelessness*, www.focusireland.ie/resource-hub/about-homelessness/.

Gosling, Paul (2018), *A New Union – Ireland 2050: A Consultative Draft Report*, self publication.

Gray, Ann Marie, Jennifer Hamilton, Gráinne Kelly, Brendan Lynn, Martin Melaugh and Gillian Robinson (2018), *The Northern Ireland Peace Monitoring Report* (Belfast: Community Relations Council).

Hayward, Kathy (n.d.) 'From Barriers to Bridges: The Europeanisation of Ireland's Borders', *CIBR Working Papers in Border Studies*.

Hederman report (Report of the Committee to Review the Offences against the State Acts 1930–1998) www.justice.ie/en/JELR/Pages/Review-of-the-Offences-against-the-State-Acts.

IMC (Independent Monitoring Commission) (2011), *Twenty-Sixth and Final Report*.

Independent Commission for the Location of Victims Remains, www.iclvr.ie.

Institute for Government (2019), www.instituteforgovernment.org.uk/explainers/irish-reunification.

Irish Council of Civil Liberties (2020), *Review of the Special Criminal Court*, www.iccl.ie/wp-content/uploads/2020/06/ICCL-Review-of-the-Special-Criminal-Court-2020.pdf.

Kelleher, Colette (blog, 03/09/19), https://colettekelleher.ie/government-using-constitution-as-excuse-to-block-housing-reform-sen-colette-kelleher/.

LSE (blog, 20/06/17), Bernadette Hayes and John Nagle, 'The Moral Guardians? DUP and Sinn Fein supporters' Attitudes to Gay and Abortion Rights', https://blogs.lse.ac.uk/politicsandpolicy/the-moral-guardians-dup-sinn-fein/.

LSE (blog, 02/11/20), Etain Tannam, 'The Shared Island Initiative is Not Just About Practical Policy, but About National Identity Post-Brexit', https://blogs.lse.ac.uk/brexit/2020/11/02/the-shared-island-project/.

Lucid Talk (2018), opinion poll, https://docs.wixstatic.com/ugd/024943_b89b42d32364461298ba5fe7867d82e1.pdf.

Lucid Talk (2020), opinion poll, www.lucidtalk.co.uk/single-post/2020/02/26/thedetail-ni-and-roi-poll-projects.

Lucid Talk (2021), opinion poll, www.lucidtalk.co.uk/single-post/lt-ni-sunday-times-january-2021-state-of-the-uk-union-poll.

McDonald, Mary Lou (YouTube, 31/01/20), 'Brexit is a Game-Changer for Irish Unity', www.youtube.com/watch?v=60zsq3jbyqw.

NIHRC (Northern Ireland human Rights Commission) (2013), 'Dealing with Northern Ireland's Past Towards a Transitional Justice Approach' (Belfast), https://nihrc.org/uploads/publications/NIHRC_Transitional_Justice_Report.pdf.

Northern Ireland Life and Times (NILT), www.ark.ac.uk/nilt/.

O'Callaghan, Margaret (2016), 'The Politics of Commemoration', Queen University blog, 23 March, http://qpol.qub.ac.uk.

Pat Finucane Centre, www.patfinucanecentre.org/collusion.

PSNI/MI5, *Paramilitary Groups in Northern Ireland*, HMSO, 19/10/15, https://assets.publishing.service.gov.uk/government/uploads/system/uploads/attachment_data/file/469548/Paramilitary_Groups_in_Northern_Ireland_-_20_Oct_2015.pdf.

Robinson, Peter, *Newsletter* (23/10/20), 'Northern Ireland needs a pro-Union group that will help prepare for any border poll', www.newsletter.co.uk/news/opinion/columnists/peter-robin

son-full-article-northern-ireland-needs-pro-union-group-will-help-prepare-any-border-poll-3012659.

Sheehan, Pat (YouTube, 07/07/20), 'Pat slams UUP leader over vile and despicable Bobby Storey tweet', www.youtube.com/watch?v=e4X_eeV7mQU.

Sinn Féin (1971), *Éire Nua*, www.leftarchive.ie/document/view/543/.

Sinn Féin (c. 1994), *Policy Document*, https://www.leftarchive.ie/document/view/1550/.

Sinn Féin (2003), *No Right Turn*, www.sinnfein.ie/contents/1021.

Sinn Fein (2007), *2007 Assembly Election Manifesto: Delivering for Ireland's Future*.

Sinn Féin (2016), *Towards an Agreed and Reconciled Future: Sinn Féin Policy on Reconciliation And Healing*, www.sinnfein.ie/files/2016/Reconciliation_Policy_Ard_Fheis_2016.pdf.

Sinn Féin (2018a), 'A National Health Service for a United Ireland', www.sinnfein.ie/files/2018/United_Ireland_Health.pdf.

Sinn Fein (2018b), Ard Fheis Clár, www.sinnfein.ie/ard-fheis-2018.

Sinn Féin (2020), 'Giving Workers & Families a Break: A Manifesto for Change', *2020 General Election Manifesto*.

Sinn Féin, *Rebuilding Stronger, Fairer, Better: Sinn Féin Alternative Budget 2021*, October 2020.

Slugger O'Toole 'Why Sinn Féin should retire Tiocfaidh ár lá ...', https://sluggerotoole.com/2020/05/06/why-sinn-fein-should-retire-tiocfaidh-ar-la/.

State of Health in the EU: Companion Report 2019, Luxembourg: Publications Office of the European Union, https://ec.europa.eu/health/sites/default/files/state/docs/2019_companion_en.pdf.

University of Liverpool, *2015 Northern Ireland General Election Survey*, www.imlab.ac.uk/politics/research/research-projects/2015-northern-ireland-general-election-survey/.

Secondary sources

Aretxaga, Begoña (2001), 'The sexual games of the body politic: fantasy and state violence in Northern Ireland', *Cult Med Psychiatry*, 25, 1–2. doi: 10.1023/A:1005630716511.

Ashe, Fidelma (2019), *Gender, Nationalism and Conflict Transformation: New Themes and Old Problems in Northern Ireland Politics* (London: Routledge).

Bean, Kevin, Keith Gildart, Brendan Lynn, Darah Buchanan, Henry Patterson, Gareth Mulvenna, Eamonn O'Kane, Paul Dixon and Christopher Norton (2010), 'Book Reviews', *Irish Political Studies*, 25:1, 135–154. doi: 10.1080/07907180903432226.

Bielenberg, Andy and Pádraig Óg Ó Ruairc (2020), 'Shallow graves; documenting & assessing IRA disappearances during the Irish revolution 1919–1923', *Small Wars & Insurgencies*. doi: 10.1080/09592318.2020.1798678.

Brown, Kris and Adrian Grant (2016), 'A lens over conflicted memory: surveying "Troubles" commemoration in Northern Ireland', *Irish Political Studies*, 31:1, 139–162. doi: 10.1080/07907184.2015.1126925.

Buckley, Fiona (2013), 'Women and politics in Ireland: the road to sex quotas', *Irish Political Studies*, 28:3, 341–359. doi: 10.1080/07907184.2013.818537.

Cairns, Ed, Frances McLernon, Ulrike Niens, Masi Noor, Aberto Voci, and Miles Hewstone (2004), 'Intergroup forgiveness and guilt in Northern Ireland: social psychological dimensions of "The Troubles"', in Nyla R. Branscombe and Bertjan Doosje (eds), *Collective Guilt: International Perspectives* (Cambridge: Cambridge University Press), 169–192.

Cassidy, Kevin J. (2005), 'Organic intellectuals and the committed community: Irish Republicanism and Sinn Féin in the North', *Irish Political Studies*, 20:3, 341–356. doi: 10.1080/07907180500359376.

Chilton, Paul (2015), 'Armed struggle, peace process and parliamentarism: James Connolly and the changing politics of Provisional Republicanism', *Australian Journal of Politics and History*, 61:4, 485–500. doi: 10.1111/ajph.12114.

Coakley, John (2017), 'Adjusting to partition: from irredentism to "consent" in twentieth-century Ireland', *Irish Studies Review*, 25:2, 193–214. doi: 10.1080/09670882.2017.1286079.

Cochrane, Mark (2013), 'Security force collusion in Northern Ireland 1969–1999: substance or symbolism?' *Studies in Conflict & Terrorism*, 36/1, 77–97.

Connolly, Tony (2018), 'A brief history of the backstop', RTÉ, 20/
10/18, www.rte.ie/news/brexit/2018/1019/1005373-backstop-
tony-connelly/.

Cooley, Laurence (2020), 'Census politics in Northern Ireland from
the Good Friday Agreement to Brexit: beyond the "sectarian
headcount"'?, *The British Journal of Politics and International
Relations*, 1–20. doi: 10.1177/1369148120959045.

Craig, Tony (2014), 'Monitoring the peace? Northern Ireland's
1975 Ceasefire Incident Centres and the politicisation of Sinn
Féin', *Terrorism and Political Violence*, 26:2, 307–319. doi:
10.1080/09546553.2012.711395.

De Bréadún, Deaglán (2015), *Power Play: The Rise of Modern Sinn
Féin* (Dublin: Irish Academic Press).

Dempster, Lauren (2016), 'The Republican Movement, "disappearing"
and framing the past in Northern Ireland', *International Journal of
Transitional Justice*, 10, 250–271. doi: 10.1093/ijtj/ijw002.

Dillenburger, Karola, Montserrat Fargas and Akhonzada, Rym
(2006), 'Victims or survivors? Debate about victimhood in
Northern Ireland', *International Journal of the Humanities*, 3:5,
222–231. doi: 10.18848/1447–9508/CGP/v03i05/41662.

Dixon, Paul (1997), 'Paths to peace in Northern Ireland: civil society and consociational approaches', *Democratization*, 4:3, 1–27.
doi: 10.1080/13510349708403513.

—— (2008), *Northern Ireland: The Politics of War and Peace*
(Basingstoke: Palgrave Macmillan).

Doyle, John and Eileen Connolly (2019), 'The effects of Brexit on
the Good Friday Agreement and the Northern Ireland Peace
Process', in Cornelia-Adriana Baciu and John Doyle (eds), *Peace,
Security and Defence Cooperation in Post-Brexit Europe: Risks
and Opportunities* (Cham: Springer International Publishing
AG), 79–96.

Dunphy, Richard (2017), 'Beyond Nationalism? The anti-austerity
social movement in Ireland: between domestic constraints and
lessons from abroad', *Journal of Civil Society*, 13:3, 267–283.
doi: 10.1080/17448689.2017.1355031.

English, Richard (2004), *Armed struggle: the history of the IRA*
(London: Pan).

Farrell, David M., Jane Suiter and Clodagh Harris (2019),
'"Systematizing" constitutional deliberation: the 2016–18

citizens' Assembly in Ireland', *Irish Political Studies*, 34:1, 113–123. doi: 10.1080/07907184.2018.1534832.

Fenton, Siobhan (2018), *The Good Friday Agreement* (Hull: Biteback Publishing).

Ferguson, Neil, Eve Binks, Micheál D. Roe, Jessica Nee Brown, Tiffany Adams, Sharon Mary Cruise and Christopher Alan Lewis (2007), 'The IRA apology of 2002 and forgiveness in Northern Ireland's Troubles: a cross-national study of printed media', *Peace and Conflict: Journal of Peace Psychology*, 13:1, 93–113. doi: 10.1037/h0094026.

Ferriter, Diarmuid (2019), *The Border: The Legacy of a Century of Anglo-Irish Politics* (London: Profile Books Ltd.).

Flynn, Kevin Haddick (1997), 'Soloheadbeg: what really happened?', *History Ireland*, 1:5, www.historyireland.com/20th-century-contemporary-history/soloheadbeg-what-really-happened/.

Gilmartin, Niall (2017), 'Feminism, nationalism and the re-ordering of post-war political strategies: the case of the Sinn Féin Women's Department', *Irish Political Studies*, 32:2, 268–292. doi: 10.1080/07907184.2016.1146698.

Grayson, Richard S. (2010), 'The place of the First World War in contemporary Irish Republicanism in Northern Ireland', *Irish Political Studies*, 25:3, 325–345. doi: 10.1080/07907184.2010.497635.

Guelke, Adrian (2014), 'Northern Ireland's flags crisis and the enduring legacy of the settler-native divide', *Nationalism and Ethnic Politics*, 20, 133–151. doi: 10.1080/13537113.2014.879770.

Hancock, Landon (2012), 'Transitional justice and the consultative group: facing the past or forcing the future?' *Ethnopolitics*, 11:2, 204–228. doi: 10.1080/17449057.2011.615594.

Hanley, Brian (2013), '"But then they started all this killing": attitudes to the I.R.A. in the Irish Republic since 1969', *Irish Historical Studies*, 38:151, 439–456.

Hannigan, John A. (1985), 'The Armalite and the ballot box: dilemmas of strategy and ideology in the Provisional IRA', *Social Problems*, 33:1, 31–40. doi: 10.2307/800629.

Hayes, Bernadette C. and Ian McAllister (2001), 'Who voted for peace? Public support for the 1998 Northern Ireland agreement', *Irish Political Studies*, 16:1, 73–93. doi: 10.1080/07907180108406633.

Hayward, Katy (2004), 'The politics of nuance: Irish official discourse on Northern Ireland', *Irish Political Studies*, 19:1, 18–38. doi: 10.1080/1356347042000269710.

—— and Mary C. Murphy (2018), 'The EU's influence on the peace process and agreement in Northern Ireland in light of Brexit', *Ethnopolitics*, 17:3, 276–291. doi: 10.1080/17449057. 2018.1472426.

—— and Cathal McManus (2019), 'Neither/Nor: the rejection of Unionist and Nationalist identities in post-Agreement Northern Ireland', *The Political Quarterly*, 43:1, 139–155. doi: 10.1177/0309816818818312.

Hearty, Kevin (2016), 'Legislating hierarchies of victimhood and perpetrators: the Civil Service (Special Advisers) Act (Northern Ireland) 2013 and the meta-conflict', *Social & Legal Studies*, 25:3, 333–353. doi: 10.1177/0964663915614887.

Hearty, Kevin (2017), *Irish Republicanism, Memory Politics and Policing* (Liverpool: Liverpool University Press).

Hopkins, Stephen (2015), 'Sinn Féin, the past and political strategy: the Provisional Irish Republican Movement and the politics of "Reconciliation"', *Irish Political Studies*, 30:1, 79–97. doi:10.10 80/07907184.2014.942293.

Kampf, Zohar (2009), 'Public (non-) apologies: the discourse of minimizing responsibility', *Journal of Pragmatics*, 41:11, 2257–2270. doi: 10.1016/j.pragma.2008.11.007.

Kelly, Stephen (2014), 'A "Southern interference in the North's affairs": the prospect of Fianna Fáil as an all-Ireland party, 1926–2011', *Irish Studies Review*, 22:4, 415–431. doi: 10.1080/ 09670882.2014.955323.

Keegan, Brian (2020), *The Sinn Féin Manifesto*, www.charteredac countants.ie/News/the-sinn-fein-manifesto.

Kinsella, Stephen (2012), 'Is Ireland really the role model for austerity?' *Cambridge Journal of Economics*, 36:1, 223–35. doi:10.1093/cje/bero32.

Lewis, Matthew and Shaun McDaid (2017), 'Bosnia on the border? Republican violence in Northern Ireland during the 1920s and 1970s', *Terrorism and Political Violence*, 29:4, 635–655. doi: 10.1080/09546553.2015.1043429.

de Londras, Fiona and Mima Markicevic (2018), 'Reforming abortion law in Ireland: reflections on the public submissions to the

Citizens' Assembly', *Women's Studies International Forum*, 70, 89–98. doi: 10.1016/j.wsif.2018.08.005.

Lundy, Patricia (2009), 'Can the past be policed? Lessons from the Historical Enquiries Team Northern Ireland', *Journal of Law and Social Challenges*, 11, 109–156.

—— and Bill Rolston (2016), 'Redress for past harms? Official apologies in Northern Ireland', *The International Journal of Human Rights*, 20:1, 104–122. doi: 10.1080/13642987.2015.1050235.

Lynch, Robert (2008), 'The people's protectors? The Irish Republican Army and the "Belfast Pogrom", 1920–1922', *Journal of British Studies*, 47:2, 375–391. doi: 10.1086/526757.

Lynn, Brendan (2005), 'The Irish Anti-Partition League and the political realities of partition, 1945–9', *Irish Historical Studies*, 34:135, 321–332. doi: 10.1017/S0021121400004508.

MacLachlan, Alice (2015), '"Trust me, I'm sorry": the paradox of public apology', *Monist*, 98:4, 441–456. doi: 10.1093/monist/onv023.

McCarthy, Mark (2012), *Ireland's 1916 Rising: Explorations of History-Making, Commemoration & Heritage in Modern Times* (London: Routledge).

McElroy, Gail (2017), 'Party competition in Ireland: the emergence of a left-right dimension?' in Gail McElroy, Michael Marsh and David Farrell (eds), *A Conservative Revolution? Electoral Change in Twenty-First Century Ireland* (Oxford Scholarship online). doi: 10.1093/acprof:oso/9780198744030.003.0005.

McGlinchey, Marisa (2019), *Unfinished Business: The Politics of 'Dissident' Irish Republicanism* (Manchester: Manchester University Press).

—— (2019), 'Does Moderation pay in a consociational democracy? The marginalisation of the SDLP in the North of Ireland', *Swiss Political Science Review*, 25:4, 426–449. doi: 10.1111/spsr.12362.

McGrattan, Cillian (2016), 'Ideology, reconciliation and nationalism in Northern Ireland', *Journal of Political Ideologies*, 21:1, 61–77. doi: 10.1080/13569317.2016.1105407.

McGuinness, Seamus and Adele Bergin (2019), 'The political economy of a Northern Ireland border poll', IZA Discussion Paper No. 12496.

Maillot, Agnès (2005), *New Sinn Fein: Republicanism in the Twenty-First Century* (London: Routledge).

—— (2019), 'Right to work: Dáil narratives on asylum', *Studies in Arts and Humanities*, 4:2, 19–32. doi: 10.18193/sah.v4i2.139.

Meagher, Kevin (2016), *A United Ireland: Why Unification is Inevitable and how it Will Come About* (London: Biteback Publishing).

Mesev, Victor, Peter Shirlow and Joni Downs (2009), 'The geography of conflict and death in Belfast, Northern Ireland', Annals of the Association of American Geographers, 99:5, 893–903. doi: 10.1080/00045600903260556.

Murphy, Yvonne (2016), 'The Marriage Equality referendum 2015', *Irish Political Studies*, 31:2, 315–333. doi: 10.1080/079 07184.2016.1158162.

Napier, Richard J., Brendan Gallagher and Darrin Wilson (2017), 'An Imperfect Peace: Trends in Paramilitary Related Violence 20 Years After The Northern Ireland Ceasefires', *Ulster Medical Journal*, 86:2, 99–102.

Ó Broin, Eoin (2009), *Sinn Féin and the Politics of Left Wing Republicanism* (London: Pluto Press).

—— (2019), *Home: Why Public Housing is the Answer* (Dublin: Merrion Press).

O'Donnell, Catherine (2007), 'Pan-nationalism: explaining the Irish government's role in the Northern Ireland Peace Process, 1992–98', *Contemporary British History*, 21:2, 223–245. doi: 10.1080/13619460600785325.

O'Keefe, Theresa (2006), 'Menstrual blood as a weapon of resistance', *International Feminist Journal of Politics: Gender Violence and Hegemonic Projects*, 9:4, 535–556.

—— (2017), 'Policing unruly women: the state and sexual violence during the Northern Irish Troubles', *Women's Studies International Forum*, 62, 69–77. doi: 10.1016/j.wsif.2017.03.003.

O'Leary, Brendan (2018), 'The twilight of the United Kingdom & *Tiocfaidh ár lá*: twenty years after the Good Friday Agreement', *Ethnopolitics*, 17:3, 223–242. doi: 10.1080/17449057.2018.147 3114.

O'Malley, Eoin and Sean McGraw (2017), 'Fianna Fáil: the glue of ambiguity', *Irish Political Studies*, 32:1, 1–29. doi: 10.1080/07907184.2016.1271329.

O'Rourke, Catherine and Aisling Swaine (2017), 'Gender, violence and reparations in Northern Ireland: a story yet to be told', *The

International Journal of Human Rights, 21:9, 1302–1319. doi: 10.1080/13642987.2017.1360029.

O'Toole, Emer (2019), 'Panti Bliss still can't get hitched: meditations on performativity, drag, and gay marriage', *Sexualities*, 22:3, 359–380. doi: 10.1177/1363460717741809.

Power, Martin J., Amanda Haynes and Eoin Devereux (2016), 'Reasonable people vs. the sinister fringe', *Critical Discourse Studies*, 13:3, 261–277. doi: 10.1080/17405904.2016.1141694.

Puirséil, Niamh (2017), 'Fianna Fáil and the evolution of an ambiguous ideology', *Irish Political Studies*, 32:1, 49–71. doi: 10.1080/07907184.2016.1269755.

Rankin, J.K. (2006), 'The Provenance and Dissolution of the Irish Boundary Commission', *Working Papers in British-Irish Studies*, 79, www.ucd.ie/ibis/filestore/wp2006/79/79_kr.pdf.

Savage, M., T. Callan, B. Nolan and B. Colgan (2019), 'The great recession, austerity and Inequality: lessons from Ireland', *The Review of Income and Wealth*, 65:2, 312–336. doi: 10.1111/roiw.12337.

Scull, Maggie (2020), 'The Troublesome World of Paramilitary Funerals', RTÉ Brainstorm, 8 July, www.rte.ie/brainstorm/2020/0708/1151996-northern-ireland-paramilitary-funerals-troubles-bobby-storey-provisional-ira/.

Shanahan, Timothy (2009), *The Provisional Irish Republican Army And The Morality Of Terrorism* (Edinburgh: Edinburgh University Press).

Smyth, Marie (2009), 'Hierarchies of pain and responsibility: victims and war by other means in Northern Ireland', *Trípodos*, 25, 27–40.

Somerville Ian and Shane Kirby (2012), 'Public relations and the Northern Ireland peace process: dissemination, reconciliation and the "Good Friday Agreement" referendum campaign', *Public Relations Inquiry*, 1:3, 231–255. doi: 10.1177/2046147X12448370.

Swaine, Aisling (2018), *Conflict-Related Violence against Women: Transforming Transition* (Cambridge: Cambridge University Press).

Taylor Rupert (2009), 'The injustice of a consociational solution to the Northern Ireland problem', in Rupert Taylor (ed.), *Consociational Theory: McGarry and O'Leary and the Northern Ireland Conflict* (London: Routledge), 309–330.

Trommer, Silke (2019), 'Watering down austerity: scalar politics and disruptive resistance in Ireland', *New Political Economy*, 24:2, 218–234. doi: 10.1080/13563467.2018.1431620.

Virdee, Satnam and Brendan McGeever (2018), 'Racism, crisis, Brexit', *Ethnic and Racial Studies*, 41:10 (2018), 1802–1819. doi: 10.1080/01419870.2017.1361544.

Wahidin Azrini and Jason Powell (2017), '"The Irish conflict" and the experiences of female ex-combatants in the Irish Republican Army: power, resistance and subjectivity', *International Journal of Sociology and Social Policy*, 37:9/10 (2017), 555–571. doi: 10.1108/IJSSP-05-2016-0052.

White, Robert W. (1997), 'The Irish Republican Army: an assessment of sectarianism', *Terrorism and Political Violence*, 9:1 (1997), 20–55. doi: 10.1080/09546559708427385.

Index